GALLOPING AROUND THE COSMOS

MEMORIES OF TV'S WAGON TRAIN TO THE STARS FROM TODAY'S GROWN-UP KIDS

Becky BOOKS

GALLOPING AROUND THE COSMOS
Memories of TV's Wagon Train to the Stars from Today's Grown-Up Kids
Copyright © 2023 by Jim Beard

Becky Books and the Becky Books Logo © Jim Beard

Introduction © 2023 by Jim Beard
All essays © 2023 their respective authors

Cover illustration by Ron Hill
Cover logo, interior layout, and formatting by Maggie Ryel

This book is not affiliated with or endorsed by CBS Studios, Paramount Pictures, or any other entity past or present officially connected with *Star Trek* and any other properties discussed in this book.

ISBN: 9798861630771

First Edition

For the Little Woman, who once got to adore William Shatner from afar (about ten or so feet) and said 'twas enough.
Jim Beard

THE TURBOLIFT

My Star Track Will Go On Forever – An Introduction 1
Jim Beard

An Obsession Most Welcome 5
Alex Segura

Beach Blanket Chekov 12
Nancy Holder

My Piece of the Action 18
Tom K. Mason

The Home on the Edge of Forever 25
Jeff "Venture" Fournier

Bob's Personal Log 32
Robert Greenberger

Growing Up in that Forgotten Space Sector:
The Finger Lakes 38
Ed Catto

Giant-Size *Trek* Thing 48
Rich Handley

Mrs. Mallon's Enterprise 57
John S. Drew

My Early Treks with Captain Kurt 65
Alan J. Porter

A Game for the Young 73
Bobby Nash

I Wasn't a Teenage *Star Trek* Fan 82
Tom Brevoort

Captain's Log, Star Date: Fourth Gradee 89
John C. Bruening

To Boldly Go 96
Ron Hill

Scare Trek 100
Greg Cox

And the Child Shall Trek Forever More 107
Dayton Ward

A Voice in the Wilderness 115
Van Allen Plexico

The Derek in the Dark 123
Derek Tyler Attico

My Sunday Mornings at 10:00 AM 130
Gordon Dymowski

Sunshine and Sci-Fi 138
Corinna Bechko

Saturdays and Starships 145
Aaron Smith

**This is What Happens When You
Start Watching *Star Trek* From Birth** 153
Keith R.A. DeCandido

Confessions of a *Star Trek* Non-Fan Fan 159
Paul Kupperberg

The Tapestry of *Trek* 166
Andrew Leyland

The *Enterprise* Influence 176
Michael A. Gordon

Boldly Bits and Pieces 183
Sorella Smith

Acknowledgments 191

MY STAR TREK WILL GO ON FOREVER

AN INTRODUCTION

BY JIM BEARD

Like *Star Trek* itself, this book contains action and adventure, philosophy and poetry, fancy and flight, and, most important of all, light and darkness.

That's important for me to stress here at the beginning, because I'm sure there will be many preconceived notions of what this book offers, some of them most likely formed by my own back-cover copy. That's all great; no worries here, but if we did our jobs right, this book also offers some surprises. I think you'll know them when you reach those moments, and I think you'll agree with me that they embrace the underlying tenets of *Star Trek*, most specifically "Infinite Diversity in Infinite Combinations."

My own childhood *Trek* memories might illustrate this point. One of the earliest of them is an argument I had with my own siblings, one that's stayed with me my entire life.

Flashback to the very early 1970s, perhaps even the actual year of 1970. *Star Trek* was in its first syndication, and that's how I became a fan. I was barely over a year old when it debuted in '66, and I'm pretty sure I don't have any clear recollections of watching episodes first-run. No, my *Star Trek* fandom grew out of watching it on Sundays on whatever station was showing it (no idea). I do recall thinking it was new at that time, something I pretty much did for all TV shows, still too young to dope out the whole syndication/reruns thing.

The argument? Well, every summer my parents took me and my

brother and sister to a big amusement park only an hour away from my hometown, and on this one occasion, riding in my dad's powder-blue Ford station wagon, we kids spotted a billboard advertising, what else, *Star Trek*.

Now, I don't know the hows and whys of it, I only know what I know. Some station or whatnot was promoting their airing of *Trek* on a billboard and my siblings spotted it and remarked upon it.

Me, little ol' five or six-year-old me, immediately pounced on that and corrected them. "Star *Track*," I told them. "There's no such word as *trek*."

Yes, not one of my proud childhood proclamations. I was precocious and precious, of course, but also somewhat naïve. My brother and sister, four and five years older than me, respectively, pounced back and ripped me to shreds. The wounds from that altercation have never truly healed, a good portion of which is due to the fact that the two of them didn't let me forget my stupidity for years to come.

For the record, the show is called *Star* Trek.

The darkness didn't end there. Not too long after that unfortunate gaffe, I was watching the show, "The *Enterprise* Incident," in fact, and at the coda, when McCoy calls Kirk down to sickbay to have his temporary pointed ears "bobbed," my sister, who was never a fan of the show or even science fiction in general, asked why they couldn't just do the same for Spock's ears.

Yeah, I hear you.

I sputtered, I shook, I quaked, a veritable hurricane of indignation and incredulity welling up inside me. *Now* who was being *stupid*, I thought and then attempted to explain how ignorant she was—but words failed me (and me a budding writer!) and she walked away, never really understanding the damning faux pas she'd made. To this day, my sister still doesn't understand.

Not all my *Star Trek* childhood memories are like these. I remember embracing the show as my love for science fiction grew and grew in those days. I remember becoming obsessed with the design of the *Enterprise* and drawing it every chance I could, even risking the wrath of my art teachers at Saturday art museum classes. I remember sitting in front of the TV in my dad's La-Z-Boy recliner, waiting for the show to come on, my *The Making of Star Trek* paperback at the ready for me to look up the episode the very second the title card appeared on the screen.

I remember my frustration and confusion when some of the episodes weren't in my book, not realizing it was originally published before the third season aired. It took me a while to figure that one out.

If you recall, I was the kid who didn't believe the word *trek* existed.

My point here, and it can't be bobbed away like Kirk's phony Romulan ears, is that *Star Trek* encompasses many, many things—good and bad, dark and light, love and hate—and you're going to see them all in this book. The essays here are journeys, not unlike those of the Good Ship *Enterprise*, and the emphasis is on those combinations and diversities. There are common threads here, yes, which to me is such a wonderful thing, but there is also individuality, which is also so wonderful. It speaks to the show's mission. It speaks to its unique voice in science fiction.

If we did our jobs well, you're going to see not only yourself here, but the entire universe of possibilities.

There's another story here, too.

I went to see *Star Trek II: The Wrath of Khan* with my dad on its first day, first screening. In the darkened theater, at the auspicious, sobering moment of Jim Kirk separated from his dying friend Spock, unable to get to him, hearing only his final words, I was taken out of the moment by the sounds of someone crying.

Tearing my eyes from the historical scene on the screen, I looked around and spotted a figure in a seat a few rows in front of me. The person—I could see then it was a girl—was sobbing, her grief loud enough for me to hear it and bring me out of my own sadness over Spock's death. I remember shaking my head at it, not cruelly, simply thinking to myself there were all kinds of people in the world, and some of them really loved *Star Trek*.

Six years later, I met a girl who would, a year after that, become my wife. It was, I believe, one of our first long conversations and the subject of *Trek* came up. We began to talk about how we would both go to the first day of new movies, and I related the above story to her.

Becky looked at me, verified date and time, and said, "That was me."

Over the following years we realized how many times we'd been in the same place around the same time before we actually met in person, but I treasure the story of "the girl who cried for Spock" because I feel that's the first time I met Becky and truly knew her heart. It is of absolutely no surprise to me that I wanted to be her husband after her revelation to me of that day in 1982.

Becky is gone now, off on her own star trek, but I keep her love for the show in my own heart and recollections, as well as honoring her memory with this book (and Becky Books in general). It was her most favorite show of all, and one of the most significant moments in her life concerning it is when she was in the middle of a very, very dark time and, feeling herself in danger, focused on the crew of the *Enterprise*, of their light and their ability to save anyone at any time. Incredibly, her *Trek* fandom got her through that time.

Dark and light, light and dark. This won't be the last time you see those forces at work in this book, but I promise you there's always light at the end of the tunnel.

Because that's what *Star Trek* is all about. And my personal star track will go on forever. Here's hoping yours will, too.

Beyond
The rim of the star-light
My love
Is wand'ring in star-flight

Jim Beard
September 2023

AN OBSESSION MOST WELCOME

BY ALEX SEGURA

I didn't think I had room for another hobby, much less another all-consuming, immersive obsession. But we don't decide those things. They just happened.

Strangely enough, my lifelong love of *Star Trek* didn't start with the show. I was aware of it, of course. I had a vague idea of what *Star Trek* was as a pre-teen. But I was busy—as busy as kids get, I suppose. I was obsessed with comics, cartoons, and football. And I lived in Miami, a literal tropical paradise that was rife with distractions.

My first real, concrete moment with Trek didn't even happen in front of a television screen. It was at my local comic shop, a few blocks from my dad's house. I'd wandered over with a few bucks to spare, desperate for the new issue of *Uncanny X-Men* or what-have-you. The place was cramped, musty-smelling, and the kind of spot you could lose yourself in. It's what I did. My parents had just gotten divorced. I was a shy, bookish kid trying to find my way. Books, comics, and television were the escape valve. A way to disconnect from the things going on outside of me that I couldn't control.

I did my usual thing. Grabbed the comics on my list, wandered the store, rifled through the back issue bins. But this trip was different. As I paid for my items, the owner looked at me and asked, "You like *Star Trek*?"

I said yes, even though, honestly, I wasn't sure. I mean, of course I liked it, this thing I didn't know anything about. It *sounded* cool, right?

Before I finished my response, the owner turned around and started rummaging through a box behind the counter. He came back and dropped a smaller box next to my stack of comics. *Star Trek* OFFICIAL TRADING CARDS.

"Want 'em?"

I said yes before fully thinking through what it meant. The box went into my bag, and I was gone, wondering just what I'd accepted.

I didn't have to wait long. When I got back to my dad's, he was busy watching *SportsCenter*, and the rest of the family was out shopping. I set up in my dad's office and started to carefully open each of the packs of cards. What I found blew my mind.

Now, as a brief aside, these cards came in two sets: TOS and TNG. They were timed to the show's 25th anniversary, and not only featured cards on each episode, but also character-specific ones as well. It was, for a kid obsessed with trading cards—Marvel, sports, or whatever—the perfect springboard into the franchise.

Hours passed like minutes. I learned about the dashing and brave Captain James T. Kirk. The mysterious and aloof Mr. Spock. Gruff and lovable Dr. McCoy. The serene and insightful Lieutenant Uhura. I couldn't stop reading. I visited the planet Vulcan. I watched as the ship went where no one had gone before. I marveled at the Enterprise itself and immersed myself in the details: which uniform color matched what branch of Starfleet, what the Federation was, things like the Prime Directive, warp drives, dilithium crystals, "The City on the Edge of Forever," and so much more. It was a crash course in a world that felt like it'd been waiting for me.

Hours later, as I heard my family returning home from their adventures, I realized the cards wouldn't be enough. I'd downloaded the basic info, but I needed to *feel* the story. I needed to experience this thing called *Star Trek*. I, too, wanted to go where no one had gone before. I wanted to be aboard the Enterprise. I wanted to hear these characters speak to each other. It all felt very tentative—sure, the info on these cards sounded really neat and engaging. But would the show itself hold up?

I wouldn't have to wait long to find out. A few nights later, in bed at my *abuelos'* house, the clock ticked past midnight. I flipped through the channels. Past *Saturday Night Live*. Past the evening news or late-night shows. I reached the syndicated channels. I almost kept flipping until I heard what would become a familiar series of words. A monologue that would become imprinted on my memory like nothing else.

"Space...the final frontier. These are the voyages of the Starship Enterprise..."

The episode was airing in black and white. The sound on the tiny television set propped up on my dresser was crappy at best. It was late at night, and I wasn't supposed to be watching. I didn't care. This is what I'd wanted. This is what I'd hoped for. And just a few minutes into the episode—"Miri"—I was enthralled. I don't remember a lot more from that experience. I've watched the episode again many times, as part of rewatches of the entire series. But something magical happened that night. My theoretical brain—the part of my mind that knew *Star Trek* was for me—merged with my heart, with the part of my soul that experienced that episode and just wanted *more*. Wanted to be on the Enterprise bridge. Wanted to learn about where Spock came from. Wanted to spend time with Kirk, McCoy, Sulu, and Scotty.

Like any good fiction, it was about the characters. The people. They felt real—thoughtful, complicated, heroic. The show boasted an all-star cast, a collection of actors delivering material in unmatched ways. But the young reader in me—and future writer—also appreciated something else. The ambition. For a better world. The chance to see that things might not be terrible in the future. The idea that we might get our lives together and find a softer, better way of living, a universe driven by peace and brotherhood, by the desire for knowledge. Not driven by hate, racism, war, and anger. It felt so novel and refreshing. And good. Starfleet was not a military branch of the government. The Enterprise was not a warship. It was a scientific expedition, meant to educate and inform the galaxy about what lay beyond known space. It was thrilling and evocative, and even at my young age, I could see the allegories that commented on the world we lived in today, even if the show itself was then twenty-five years old.

And wow, the writing. Sharp, complex, character-driven, and loaded with new ideas. Every episode felt like it was propelling me, the viewer, into a new universe with new rules, aliens, backstories, and conflicts. I couldn't get enough. I couldn't stop.

But unlike today, where you can literally say the name of the show you want to see and it'll be presented to you on a silver platter, television was quite different then. For whatever reason, *Star Trek* wasn't being syndicated in prime time in Miami, aside from *The Next Generation* spinoff. But even at that nascent stage in my Trek fandom, I knew I was a TOS guy. As much as I love all iterations of the idea, I would always gravitate first to the original. And that's what I wanted to see. Saturdays at 11:30pm became appointment television for me, snuggled up in bed, eyes glued to the tiny screen across the room, volume down low enough not to disturb anyone else but loud enough for me to hear. It was a religious experience, and the kind of thing that required dedication and focus on my part. I needed that dose of Trek each week to add fuel to the fire burning in my mind. Details about characters. New alien races to ponder. Rules and concepts I hadn't even considered. But soon, even that wasn't enough.

I was already a voracious reader, of course, but the realization that there were not only books about *Star Trek*, but books set in the Trek universe opened a door that never closed. The Pocket Book novels—which were in great supply at my local library and my go-to used bookstore—helped fill the spaces between those episodes, and helped flesh out these characters that I was starting to love like friends or close family. The obsession became all-consuming, in the best way possible, and turned me on directly or secondhand to the works of writers I would follow for some time after: Harlan Ellison, Theodore Sturgeon, D.C. Fontana, Isaac Asimov (who didn't write for the show, but was part of the bigger conversation). It also lit a match for me, creatively. I wanted to be in this world of warp drives and transporter beams. I wanted to live in the heads of Kirk and Spock. I wanted to add to the chorus.

Around that time, my sixth grade English teacher, Mr. Tuohy, gave us an assignment: write a novel. We'd read a few books in class and now we'd get a chance to try to do it ourselves. We didn't have to finish, but we just had to write something longer than a few pages. I dove into the assignment with an unexpected passion. Why? Because it was a *Star Trek* novel. I spent days on the job, handwriting over one-hundred pages of a story featuring a new crew on a new ship, in the greater *Trek* universe. If it hadn't been for my terrible handwriting (I'm a left, so sue me), the B+ I ended up getting on the homework would have surely been an A. But that's not the point. What happened in that moment, with that task, was that I realized there was a path from where I was: a kid that loved stories, and particularly loved the kind of stories that were part and parcel of *Trek*, to actually writing those kinds of stories. To create the worlds I imagined and bring them to life on the page.

The original manuscript for that novel is lost to the sands of time, a victim of whatever housecleaning or reorganization struck it down at my mom's house. But the idea lives on. The energy and verve I felt while trying to add to the chorus of *Trek* episodes I'd loved lives on in me and keeps me going. Inspiration came easily to me because I was so immersed in the world. I wanted to be in this bright, optimistic future Gene Roddenberry created. It's a debt I can never repay and something I think about often.

Now, here's the hard part. Summing up in a few sentences what a pop culture behemoth like *Star Trek* meant to me. I could go on and on, I guess, about the cerebral—itemizing the great plot twists, the meaningful performances, the magnificent world-building that is just endemic to *Star Trek: The Original Series*—but that would feel slightly disingenuous. For me, my first encounter with *Trek* was a primal thing. It felt very much like finding something I was meant to discover. And thinking back on those early days, the memories relating to *Trek* are almost flashes - visions of experiences. Dreamlike vignettes.

The shock of Gary Mitchell's fate at the conclusion of "Where No Man Has Gone Before."

The wonder and majesty of "Journey to Babel."

The terror as I watched Spock and Kirk face off on Vulcan in "Amok Time."

The bonkers energy of "Spock's Brain."

The loopy, dark terror of the series finale, "Turnabout Intruder."

The heart-wrenching choices made in "The City on the Edge of Forever."

Kirk whispering the secrets of shield access codes to Saavik in *Star Trek II: The Wrath of Khan*, and the film's haunting final moments between him and Spock.

Reading a battered copy of Peter David's TOS novel, *The Rift*, while shivering in fear as Hurricane Andrew battered Miami, destroying swaths of homes and leaving us all forever changed.

Sitting alone in a half-empty theater, watching Captain Kirk's final moments in *Star Trek: Generations*.

Star Trek was part of me. And continues to be. It informs my life, my worldview, and my hopes for the future. It's taught me how to be a better writer, but also how to be a better person, a truer friend. *Star Trek*, at its best, gives you hope but doesn't undersell reality, that we will always have challenges, there will always be conflict, there will always be hate and rage. But we can approach those things with hope in our hearts, and with an open hand instead of a closed fist. My kids know I'm in a good mood when I'm whistling the *Star Trek* theme. It's just a part of who I am.

What if I hadn't gotten that box of cards? What if I hadn't flipped on the television that Saturday night? What if Mr. Tuohy had just assigned us to read something else? Life is a series of variables and roads not taken, and I'm grateful for the paths I did choose—or those that chose me. Without them, I certainly wouldn't be a writer today. My first sci-fi novel hits next year, and it's very much a love letter to Trek and the world those characters live in. There's no way it'd be possible or exist if not for the events outlined here, and I wouldn't have it any other way.

Live long and prosper.

Alex Segura is an acclaimed and bestselling author of novels and comics. Secret Identity, his comic book noir novel, won the LA Times Book Prize in the mystery/thriller category and has been nominated for the Anthony, Lefty, Barry, and Macavity Awards. He is also the author of *Star Wars: Poe Dameron: Free Fall, Araña/Spider-Man 2099: Dark Tomorrow*, the Pete Fernandez Quintet of mystery novels, and various comic books, including stories featuring characters like Superman, Spider-Man, the X-Men, Avengers, Moon Knight, Green Lantern, Archie, and many of his own creations. A Miami native, he lives in New York with his wife and two children. You can find him at www.alexsegura.com.

BEACH BLANKET CHEKOV

BY NANCY HOLDER

My early days were rich with visiting strange new worlds. When I was eleven, my blended family of one half-sister, a full sister, two stepsisters, a step-grandmother, my stepmother, and my father flew from San Diego to Yokosuka, Japan to live for three years. "We" were in the Navy, and my father, a psychiatrist, was transferred to the base naval hospital. There he tended to sailors dealing with the horrors of the VietNam War. Our newspaper, *The Stars and Stripes*, censored so much of what was going on in the States, and weirdly (to grown-up me, but not teen me), the new kids on base (families were forever being transferred to Japan and/or back to the States) never told us much about the larger issues of the day. Mostly we girls talked about granny dresses, skorts, Eggnog Grog lipstick, and the Beatles. We watched Japanese TV and the closest thing we had to American programming was *Batman* (the Adam West series) dubbed in Japanese.

When I was fourteen, we returned to the States. We came home on a cruise ship, the *President Wilson*, docking in San Francisco. The *Wilson* carried our Greenbriar van in its hold. The first thing we did was climb in, roll up the windows and lock the doors, and drive through Haight Ashbury. There were hippies *everywhere*. Topless guys in bellbottom jeans with hair down to the small of their backs stood on street corners and played flutes and guitars. A trio of girls with feathers braided into their hair dipped and pranced past shops festooned with swirly signs. Restaurants seemed to be serving nothing but brown rice and falafel. My stepmother yelled, "DON'T ROLL DOWN THE WINDOWS!"

We were agog. What had been going on over here?

Shortly after this jarring arrival in the States, I went by myself to visit my cousins in Redondo Beach, California. Redondo Beach was and still is an upscale beach community in Los Angeles county; back then it was the quintessential Beach Boys endless summer surfer town, as romanticized in movies like *Beach Blanket Bingo*, which had I had seen at the base movie theater back in Yokosuka despite my stepmother's protests that with a title like that, it was not appropriate. After all, there was a character named Eric Von Zipper... It never dawned on me to wonder how Annette Funicello and Frankie Avalon could party all summer without jobs or, apparently, parents. I just knew they were cool. I knew they had fun. I knew I wasn't like them.

My oldest cousin was also cool. He owned a woody station wagon and later a Porsche, and he drove my two girl cousins and me up and down the strip by the beach and laughed at me because I thought there was a singer named Ikentina Turner and I didn't know most of the Top Ten songs on the radio. I had never heard any of the Viet-Nam War protest songs. I hadn't even known there were protests. "You're going to have to catch up," he informed me. "Fast."

Even worse, my older girl cousin, who owned three hundred dollars' worth of Mary Quant makeup and worked at Judy's, a hip clothing store chain, had to cart me around when she wanted to hang out with her friends. I knew I was embarrassing her. I had the wrong clothes. I had bad hair. Her friends drank. I didn't. Some of them even smoked. And they knew she was stuck with me until I left.

It was all too much. I was a stranger in a strange land, and that strange land was the land of my birth. Like my homesick father, I yearned to go back to Japan.

Until one fateful day when, for some reason, I was alone at the Redondo Beach house with my aunt, and she announced that it was time to watch *Star Trek*. She assembled a home version of Chex Party Mix and grabbed us a couple of bottles of 7Up, and we sat down together on the couch. She clicked on the TV.

And I forgot about Ikentina Turner, and bad hair, and embarrassing my cousin, and missing "home," because I was on the *Enterprise* with Captain Kirk and his crew. And what a crew. For one thing, unlike Japanese television, *Star Trek* was in color! And it was hip! It even featured Lt. Uhura, a gorgeous Black woman (whom

I mixed up at first with Diahann Carroll, who was the first Black woman to headline a sitcom, in this case, *Julia*. There was so much television, and in English! I had to catch up, fast.)

The stories were unusual and intriguing. The crew was always beaming down to planets in twinkling disintegration scenes (wow!) and figuring out that there were problems with the dilithium crystals and/or the tribbles. And solving them all by the end of the show. It was exciting, but not too exciting. And it was comforting. Everything ended happily, at least for the crew, or you knew they would eventually be okay (Kirk swooned and/or grieved over unattainable women now and then.) Cozy science fiction! No wonder my aunt liked *Star Trek*!

And the best part of all of this wonderfulness was Ensign Chekov.

Ah, Chekov, with his Monkees Davy Jones/Beatles haircut and his cool Russian accent. "Kiptin Kirk!" I didn't know the word "naïve" but to me, he was kind of innocent and plucky, and although the older, wiser crew members were amused by him and might even chuckle when he mispronounced something or bragged about Russia, they never laughed at him. Watching Chekov, I realized that you/one/I could not know everything about America (because the *Enterprise* seemed like America to me) and still be part of the gang. You could mispronounce words ("wessels"/"Ike and Tina") and you could still save the world/restore the time-warp continuum. *And* you could still be cute!

I "followed" Chekov as I continued to watch *Star Trek*. I saw TOS through his eyes, basically. I developed my lifelong trick of focusing in on one person/character/actor to figure out something new. Later on in life, Seahawk/Forty-Niner cornerback Richard Sherman taught me about football; artist Sandro Botticelli showed me Renaissance Italy; Emperor Commodus guided me through the glory of Ancient Rome.

But Chekov was my Yoda, and he taught me life lessons about fitting in and getting along even when you didn't know the ground rules. *Star Trek* was all about finding your way. Sure, the entire crew sniped and quarreled (just like my blended family), but they worked out their differences (unlike my blended family) and persuaded the populations of whole planets to be nicer to each other, or they saved beautiful space princesses, or shared a good laugh at something not just Chekov but even the higher-ranked Mr. Spock said.

Like Chekov, Spock rarely got the joke on the first chuckle. Ah, Spock, perpetual outsider, who should have been my avatar. But to my teen eyes, he was kinda old. So, my allegiance stayed with Chekov, and *Star Trek* episodes saved my Redondo Beach summer vacation. I asked my cousin to do my hair. I learned the songs of the Top Ten. And I kept watching *Trek* with my aunt.

Then there was another jolt on my ongoing mission: tenth grade. In Japan, at Nile C. Kinnick High School in Yokohama, ninth graders were on the bottom rung of the social ladder. But in Vista, California, where we moved so my father could commute to his new tour of duty at Camp Pendleton, high school started with tenth grade. So, I had to start over, and I panicked. I forgot my *Trek* lessons: I couldn't go to Judy's for school clothes; the haircut I got in Redondo Beach had grown out... I stood alone in the Vista High cafeteria (my stepsisters and I were not hanging out) with my lunch, staring at all the unfamiliar faces, trying to figure out where to sit.

And then I met Janet and Margaret, names changed to protect the innocent.

They were *Star Trek* fans.

They were delighted to meet a fellow *Star Trek* fan.

For months, we spent our lunchtimes together and talked about the show. They agreed that I could "have" Chekov. Janet wanted Spock. I don't remember who Margaret got (I assume Kirk), but we each had our own guy. We "owned" them in some odd but very fun and comforting way, possessively, and we dressed them up in adventures of our devising, treating them almost like the Annette and Frankie Avalon of space travel. We talked about episodes; we embellished them, fixed them. We told complex stories about our Trek guys to each other. I didn't realize it at the time, but I was learning how to become a writer.

We'd bring our lunches rather than buying in the cafeteria so that we would have more time to natter on about *Trek*. I was acutely aware that this set us apart and made us oddballs, but *Star Trek*, already my cornerstone of reassurance, was bigger than the holy grail of teen popularity, and after all, we three had each other. *Star Trek* had been my landing spot during the summer of Ikentina Turner and was now my salvation from the threat of future lunch tray moments.

I did some research for this essay and learned that the powers that be decided to increase Chekov's visibility in season three. But by the broadcast of "Spectre of the Gun," the sixth episode of the third season, in which Chekov has a romance and appears to die, I had a real live boyfriend. So, Chekov, while appealing (okay, adorable), was no longer the (sole) focus of my teen gaze. I want to tell you that after I got a boyfriend, I still had lunch with my *Star Trek* girlfriends and that we kept up with our *Star Trek* storytelling, but in the ways of teenage girls in the sixties, I spent nearly all my lunches with my real, live guy. Since acquiring a boyfriend was a sign of teen success back then, I felt like I had finally figured out how to maneuver life in the States. I still watched *Trek*, and I hung out with Janet, as she was my BFF, but we no longer "played" *Star Trek* when we got together. I eventually lost track of Margaret when the semester ended and my lunch period changed, no longer coinciding with hers.

But when asked to write this essay, and casting back to that summer of *Star Trek*, I remembered those days with a nostalgic fondness that overshadowed the faded realization that I really *needed Star Trek*. What I didn't tell you at the beginning of this essay was that my mother died when I was two weeks shy of ten; my father asked two women at the same time to marry him before I turned eleven. (Only one said yes.) A year later, my big new family moved to Japan. When I was sixteen, I dropped out of high school to study ballet in Germany, and six weeks later my father died. My stepmother prevented me from returning to Germany until I graduated from high school, which I did, getting away from home as soon as possible.

I didn't want all that to overshadow my story of finding *Trek*, because to me, that life was normal life. I didn't realize quite how traumatic it was until it was over. All I knew back then was that I wanted to fit in, and have friends, and be accepted for who I was. And that all happened. And it is my life today. I love, and am loved, and I truly think I owe my insights into how to do that to my *Star Trek* summer, and most specifically to Pavel Chekov, who was "my" guy. So, live long and prosper, my dear old friend.

Just like I did, and still do to this day.

Thanks to *Trek*.

Nancy Holder is a *New York Times* bestselling author who has written dozens of novels and hundreds of short stories. She is known for writing material for *Buffy the Vampire Slayer*, *Teen Wolf*, and other TV shows, and she has novelized movies such as Gal Gadot's *Wonder Woman* and *Crimson Peak*. She has received Lifetime Achievement awards from the Horror Writers Association and the International Association of Media Tie-In Writers, and she is a Baker Street Irregular. For several years she wrote and co-wrote monthly columns for the Science Fiction and Fantasy Writers of America publications. She is currently writing the comic books *Johnny Fade* and *They Call Me Midnight* with Alan Philipson.

MY PIECE OF THE ACTION

BY TOM K. MASON

My love of *Star Trek* started because my mother hoped I'd broken my leg. That's something that would at least make the drive to the ER worth her time.

Perhaps I should back up a little.

I saw one episode of the original *Star Trek* TV show when it aired in prime time. Then I didn't see another episode until many years later when they were all syndicated and I was watching them after-the-fact.

I thank my leg every time the cold weather makes it tingle. If I hadn't hurt my leg, I'd never have seen an episode of *Star Trek* during its original network run.

Here's the beginning to all of that.

I used to ride my bike to school on most days when the weather allowed it. I loved it because it let me set my own schedule without worrying about catching the bus. I could also get home quicker. School let out at 3:20, and with luck I could be home by 3:30 and catch whatever was on TV.

That was usually the rest of *Bewitched*, *Gilligan's Island*, and then *The Early Show*. That was a 4:30 movie block that showed genre movies like *King Kong*, *Tarzan*, *Charlie Chan*, and others. In the three-channel world of 1960s television, and my parents only having two channels, having a run of shows I wanted to watch was a goldmine.

One afternoon, I was leaving school way too fast and holding on to too many things. I'm sure people might've said to me to slow down or carry fewer things or be careful. I was not yet a teenager, but I knew I wasn't listening to any voices of concern.

My bike was a metallic lime green Huffy knock-off of the classic Spyder bike. It was a little bigger, a little heavier, and I could sit on it like I was on a Harley. I didn't know how to sit on a Harley, of course, and had never been on one, but I'd seen several people sit that way on TV.

My bike didn't have a basket, and backpacks weren't cool yet, so I was carrying my textbooks with one hand and steering with the other. Here's the irony of it all. I never did homework at home, so carrying the books back and forth was really just for show. I could've easily left them in my locker like I did on most days.

My feet somehow tangled in the bike's frame, and I fell off. I wasn't even twenty-five feet from the school's front door. Everyone who saw this was very amused. For a few moments, I was the school's accidental equivalent of Buster Keaton. My leg hurt just enough that I had to walk my bike home. Worse, I was now going to be late for my afternoon TV.

Obviously, the saddest day ever.

When I got home, I did what I always did. Since my father was at work, I sat sideways in his official "dad chair." With a Diet Pepsi and a bag of Fritos, I settled in for the next couple of hours. I couldn't have been happier. Weekday afternoon TV was all I needed.

I didn't think about my leg for a while because Gilligan thought there was a ghost haunting the island and some hijinks were ensuing.

By the time dinner was ready, however, I could barely walk to the table. My knee really hurt from the fall.

There was concern all around.

"Maybe just walk it off." That was my dad. "Walking it off" was his suggestion for many childhood injuries where the bone wasn't poking through the skin.

"I hope it's not broken!" That was my mom. It was delivered more as a warning about how my leg might ruin dinner and put the family's weekend plans into some kind of disarray.

After much adult hand-wringing, my mom made me run through a list of everything that was wrong, every ache and pain in my leg, and to show her where on my knee it hurt.

Then she called our family doctor at his home.

How small a town is that? Before the town's healthcare infrastructure was overrun by insurance companies and HMOs, there was a time when a concerned parent could call the family doctor at his house at dinner time. And that doctor would answer. I thought that was normal because I'd also seen that on TV reruns.

My mom rattled off my list of symptoms, then hung up.

"We have to drive all the way to Radford for x-rays," she announced. "So, I hope it's worth it!"

I still don't know what that meant. Did she want it to be severe enough to make it worth the time and effort to get an x-ray? Would she be happy or disappointed if I wasn't seriously injured?

Radford was about twenty miles away and the only town in the area that had a hospital. After dinner, my sister went to bed, a last-minute sitter came over, and my mom and dad drove me to the hospital.

I had never been to a hospital before as a patient. My grandmother was a nurse's aide, so I'd seen the inside of the big city hospital where she worked. I'd also seen hospitals on TV. This was my first visit to a rural hospital. This was exciting, except for the pain.

At the hospital, I was checked in and we waited. I didn't mind the wait. I thought to bring a book with me. Comics were still devalued then so I didn't dare bring them with me to a public place.

A rural hospital at night is a weirdly creepy place. Dimmed lights, long corridors, odd wall color choices and a limited staff gave the hospital a post-apocalyptic horror movie feel, although I hadn't seen a post-apocalyptic horror movie by then.

I was soon wheeled to the x-ray room. An attendant took pictures of my knee from different angles and wheeled me out. While we waited for the images to be developed and for a doctor to look at them, my dad read the book he'd brought and smoked a cigarette. You could do both in a hospital in those days. My mother paced, clucked her tongue against the roof of her mouth, exhaled loudly, and asked anybody who walked by "What's taking so long?"

The reason I remember this so vividly is because this was my parents' behavior whenever they had to wait for something. Thankfully, I inherited my father's ability to kill time while waiting, except for the cigarette part.

In a scene like we've all seen in almost every TV show, the doctor came out with the x-rays. My parents and the doctor stood in the glow of the flickering overhead lights. My dad's cigarette smoke wrapped around the lights and made it look like we were in a spy show about to exchange information for nefarious purposes. I expected to see Secret Squirrel or Maxwell Smart.

The verdict was in. I had a severely stretched ligament in my left knee. There's nothing they could do about it. No tear, so there would be no surgery. No broken bones, so there wouldn't be any late-night cast-making. There wouldn't be anything for my friends to sign at school. I wouldn't be hopping up and down stairs on crutches or trying to get my parents to wait on me.

The doctor gave my mom a small container of pain pills. I was to take the pills on a regular basis, stay off my leg as much as possible, and get plenty of rest. I took one of the pills right away.

Then we were on our way back home.

I wonder if my mother considered this worth the trip.

I told that story so I could tell this one.

Driving back into town was the first time I'd seen it at night. The streets were mostly deserted, the streetlights were on, and there was an eerie *Twilight Zone* "haunted town" feeling to my hometown. That was pretty cool.

Back at home, there were some quick math calculations between my parents. My father was a scientist who could do complex equations in his head like a *Jeopardy!* champion. My mother was confused by the little dots between the big numbers on the kitchen clock.

Eventually, both agreed that if I stayed up for ninety more minutes or so, I could take another of those pain pills. The general theory was that if I was loaded up on pills before bed, there's a chance I would sleep through the night and not disturb anyone. I thought it would be great to be able to stay up later for any reason, so I remember lobbying hard for this possibility.

So, it happened. I retired to the den and our second TV, and I got to stay up late.

That's when I found *Star Trek* in its original run.

I'd never even heard of the show before. I don't remember seeing anything about it. Shows that were on past my then-bedtime were a mysterious world of adult television to me. If it was on past 8pm, I wouldn't yet know about this magical time period for another couple of years.

I'd seen the opening credits of *Perry Mason*, the old Raymond Burr show. The music to me was scary. It had to be a monster show. And Burr lumbering around a courtroom with deep set black circles for eyes had to be some kind of lawyer-Frankenstein. I never got to see an episode in those days to know how wrong I was. The reality never matched my vision of a monster lawyer. I still like my interpretation better.

I'd seen glimpses of other post-8pm shows, especially on trips to Baltimore to visit my grandparents who got ABC, a network that was as alien to my parents' TV as HBO would've been had it existed then.

But now here was something I got to see in all its cathode ray glory. *Star Trek*.

I watched the crew from the Enterprise beam down to a city that looked a lot like 1920s Earth. There were gangsters, Tommy guns, tough-talking guys in hats and pin-striped suits, laser-type weapons.

I later learned that the episode was called "A Piece of The Action" and it was written by David Harmon and Gene Coon. The Enterprise crew had arrived on the planet Sigma Iotia II to follow-up on an earlier visit by the Federation ship Horizon. As a result of contact with the Federation, Iotians became enamored with Earth's gangster era, specifically 1920s Chicago. It became their new culture, based on a book called *Chicago Mobs of the Twenties* that was left behind after contact. It was cosplay leveled up to maximum, and it was out of hand.

There were a lot of twists and turns. Kirk adopted gangster-speak to try to make a deal. He tries to teach the "gangsters" a game called Fizzbin, which for a long time I thought might be real. Spock's pointed ears were a source of conversation. There's a point at which Spock says, "Captain, you're an excellent starship commander. But as a taxi driver, you leave much to be desired." That makes me laugh even today. Scotty gets in on the fun when he references "concrete galoshes," a reinterpretation of the gangster phrase "cement shoes." Ultimately the Federation had to use some gentle force to make their point. There was even a twist ending leading to a funny tagline by Captain Kirk that recalled the episode's title: "Well, in a few years, the Iotians may demand a piece of *our* action."

It was gloriously fun and unlike anything I had seen on TV up to that time. If this was TV for adults who could stay up late, then I wanted to get my eyeballs on as much of it as possible.

I was still a kid though. When the episode was over, I took my last painkiller of the day and went to bed. On that night, *Star Trek* and I were one and done. It would be years before I saw another episode, and then I saw them all.

Paired with "The Trouble With Tribbles" written by David Gerrold, "A Piece of the Action" is my second favorite episode of the series. You can argue, obviously, that it's not the best episode of *Star Trek*, that it's not representative of the series as a whole, and that it's a weird mix of danger with quirky comedy. You can even make the case that it's kind of a bottle episode shot mostly around the Desilu backlot set that *Mission: Impossible* didn't need that week.

What you can't argue with me about is how much I love it.

That mix of science fiction with humor had a profound effect on me. It infused my own work. It led me to the books of Ron Goulart and much later to the work of John Scalzi. It also makes *Galaxy Quest* and *Star Trek IV: The Voyage Home* my favorite science fiction movies.

Years later, when I found *Star Trek* in syndication, I saw all the episodes multiple times. There are some great ones like "City On The Edge of Forever" and "Amok Time," and even the two-parter "The Menagerie." It's been pointed out that Gene Roddenberry's repurposing of his original *Star Trek* pilot created a two-part episode where the current cast of *Star Trek* watches an earlier episode of *Star Trek* on TV. That amuses me too much.

My favorite episodes of *Star Trek*, though, are still the lighthearted "funny" ones: "The Trouble With Tribbles," "Shore Leave," and of course "A Piece of the Action." They're not only the ones that I can watch repeatedly now, they're ones I recommended to my kids to give them that *Star Trek* feeling of the original series.

I've never been more grateful for a bicycle accident.

"Remember that time we drove you to the hospital for nothing," my mother would bring up years later. She has no idea how that trip affected the rest of my life.

I still think she wishes I'd broken my leg.

Tom Mason is a former comic book publishing executive (yes, that's a real job), Tom now toils on the edges of show business. He often works with animation, puppets and even some live actors. Aside from his love of *Star Trek*, he was the launch editor for Malibu Comics' *Star Trek: Deep Space Nine* comic book. Though he lives on Vancouver Island, he's been responsible for more than 600 episodes of children's entertainment as a writer, story editor and head writer for more than a dozen TV shows. Tom dabbles in book publishing as the co-author of the *Captain Awesome* books for Simon & Schuster, and the *Ella & Owen* books for Little Bee Books. He makes regular appearances on *Geekview Tavern* on YouTube, and also has a new comic book series debuting in 2024. Somewhere on his desk is his Emmy, the award he won that he can't stop talking about.

THE HOME ON THE EDGE OF FOREVER

BY JEFF "VENTURE" FOURNIER

When I was growing up *Star Trek* was akin to a religious experience, but maybe not so much in the accepted sense of the word.

We watched it after early church on Saturday night after we got home. *Every* Saturday night for over a decade or more. It was 1978 when we first watched it, and to an eight-year-old it was awesome. Canceled the same year and then blessed syndication gave us a chance for some quality sci-fi and we loved it. There was plenty on TV those days, even quite a bit of genre stuff, but *Star Trek* was a great common denominator. When we played in the fields behind our house it was exploring an alien world. We had the toy phasers eventually and many an alien monster (rabbit) was impervious to our fire. If only we had the cash for it, we would not lament our lack of communicator toys to call for a beam up.

Mom would always have dinner prepped to go when we arrived back from church Saturday evening. She put the frozen burgers in the oven broiler pan when we left and then turned on the heat when we got back. Nobody died of salmonella, and they were always perfect. Dad and the kids changed into comfortable clothes and set up the trays. Never had the *Star Trek* uniforms or even Underoos, but we figured it would be okay.

Eating in front of the television was not strictly encouraged. Tippy table trays and drinks did not go well with our Mom or the carpet. We would use metal cookie sheets on the floor and the carpet would live another decade. After Dad would set them out in the kitchen counter Mom would get the fries baking in the oven alongside the uniformly even burgers. If you have siblings, you know how important food portioning is to family peace.

Much akin to *Trek*, Mom was always an early adopter of the newest tech, especially in the kitchen. She had a metallic hand-turned burger maker for our entire lives, and I would recognize a burger made by one of those gadgets today. Her kitchen also had the newest of high-tech, a microwave oven. Dad had to order one special from a tech appliance guy he knew from his job as a telephone company repairman. Microwaves for cooking were a very new thing unless you were in the radio and electronics field. They were so new they really had not hit stores yet. We made a special family trip to the Tappan appliance store in the dead of night because Mom couldn't wait to get it when she heard it had come in. It took three of us to lift it into and out of the car, our own shuttlecraft.

Mom's embrace of the cutting-edge cooking tech was as thorough as Mr. Scott and his warp engines. She had all the manuals for the oven lined up on a shelf in the kitchen. It wasn't just that they were good resources, they were the only resources for the new way of cooking. Her first cooking action was to boil a mug of water in it for a coffee. She didn't just slavishly follow the trends either. She liked a nice egg in the morning, but microwaves tend to explode them if you whipped them up in a bowl and nuked it. After many experiments on how to make a scrambled egg in the microwave she hit upon the key: forty-four seconds on high. Not too runny and not a domestic warp core breech. Many eggs were sacrificed to science to get that data. After learning and reading recipes she would roast or bake just about anything in it. It was our own little food synthesizer in its way. After a near fire with the conventional toaster oven the microwave was king. Besides, with the toaster oven gone there was more room on the counter. Dad later made a plaque in the kitchen for Mom to go with the oven: "This is 2450-megahertz country."

(2450 MHz is the electromagnetic frequency microwaves oscillate on. We learned these things by osmosis I suppose. What other kid knew what a MASER or PHASER was? Dad always joked about building a "kid-stunning laser." I don't think it ever got past the idea stage.)

We were creative as kids and making up our own tricorders or communicators was a natural extension of our ability to create from next to nothing. Dad brought home junk control panels and operator boards from work that they were just throwing away.

The best Christmas ever was when my brother and I both got four-foot by two-foot operator cabinets Dad brought home. Sleek oak and metal that opened up. They had hundreds of lights and buttons. They even still had the wiring attached inside. We of course wanted them to light up, so Dad helped us wire them to work off nine-volt batteries. You pushed the button and it lit, you hit it again, it turned off. Later we would modify them even more to safely run off wall outlet power. We played with those things for hours and it was just light switches and imagination, just like *Star Trek*.

It was always a special Saturday night with *Trek*. We got to put whatever fixings we wanted on our burgers. Such heady freedom for a child! Cheese, mustard, and pickle was my jam. Then we would take the trays out and all sit in the living room to watch our intrepid crew. Mom thought the sci-fi shows were silly but at least they got us all together and quiet.

Dad had been a sci-fi fan since before the Air Force and his later civilian jobs of fixing TVs. He had always liked electronics and space. I didn't possess the patience for careful electronic study then. I craved adventure! Having knowledge about space was important for the future in my eyes. It was the future. I memorized the planets and carried a star map from *Astronomy Magazine* to see if I could find any of the stars mentioned in the show. We as a family were eagerly following the development of the NASA space shuttle program and loved that it was named *Enterprise*. My older brother studied the manual, and we even incorporated our junk panels into a space shuttle simulator in the basement. It had full seating for three and we could auto trigger a sound effects tape from the panels. It was a thirty-minute flight and then we could hear the wheels touchdown signaling we had landed at the end of the tape. The in-orbit portion was silent because space was a vacuum.

Trek was always coming at you from left field with relatable human drama and a future that you could see being not just possible, but probable. For pity's sake, the space shuttle would be a reality soon. We might actually survive the nuclear apocalypse we grew up expecting. The humans in *Star Trek* did. I never really felt depressed watching the show, but never a wide-eyed rose-colored view either. Their lives were just on a grander scale than ours and it seemed only inclination was all anyone lacked to change the future for the better.

For me, every week was a great time and a bit of a learning experience. We would ask Mom and Dad technical questions. "What is dilithium?" "Where is Alpha Centauri?" "Who is Gary Seven?" "Why is there in truth no beauty?" "When is the future coming?" Without the luxury of Google, Dad fielded most of the science questions and Mom would help with the practical answers. It was yet another example of their innate teamwork that would help their marriage and family stay together their entire lives. Having a tight crew was what separated the good starships from the great ones. The guiding light of logic and critical thinking was always on during Saturday night at our house. It never seemed strange to us. Everyone else was operating like aliens with strange ways. Still, it was definitely not in my character to look down on anyone. I was pretty accepting of most people except for the very cruel.

Some sparks of knowledge though were directly from the show. I was always a pretty stoic kid and the Vulcan philosophy of Infinite Diversity in Infinite Combinations (IDIC) really spoke to me. There were only amazing things to see and do in the universe, why not experience them? This helped me keep my mind always questing and learning. Thankfully, my parents valued such behavior. When I graduated from high school, I even had an IDIC pin on my robes. No one knew what it was of course, they weren't that smart about the future. I learned that my imagination was an easy to visualize thing and eventually took to drawing art as a means of expressing what was in my head. I never really appreciated my gifts and the difference they made back then. I figured everyone could do it. I was just a base line human. It was many years before I realized most people couldn't do this as easily as I.

I learned about friendship and loyalty from *Star Trek*. The main trio of characters were like a pyramid that would stand the test of time. It did create a bit of a social blind spot for me. I did not learn about when to realize a friendship was over. Much like Kirk and Garry Mitchell I was ready to be loyal to the bitter end, but a great many times friends were false. Unlike Kirk I ignored my name on the gravestone of the relationship for well past the point where I could have prepared myself. This led to a bit of an isolationist childhood compounded by my being smart and imaginative. The very same traits that made me ready for the future made my present difficult. None of the other kids seemed to watch the show.

My most fondly remembered episode is "Amok Time," as perfect a self-contained adventure as always, but it moved fast and had a visit to Vulcan. Loyalty and friendship in action, plus the exotic weapons of an alien world. "Having is not so pleasing as wanting" resonated with me as a kid for some reason. There were plenty of material things I was wanting. The family had three boys and a house, so money was always watched carefully. We made do with what we could and if we couldn't we did without. They didn't really seem to use money in the show, and they never seemed to lack for anything. That sounded like a neat system, but probably not realistic in the real world. What would T'Pring even get from marrying Spock? They certainly didn't support each other emotionally. Perhaps it was a status thing.

There were a lot of complex subjects that went over my head in that episode. Why did Spock need to go to Vulcan just to get married? Kirk could do marriages on the Enterprise. Just call her up and get the job done over a subspace radio. They could meet up later and have a honeymoon onboard ship. It would have been really nice. I was such a romantic as a kid. The whole biological drive thing was lost on me as a child. It was a weirdly alien culture but seemed pretty consistent, so I suspended disbelief, "jingle bell" frames and all.

Trek was good at getting you to suspend disbelief while simultaneously getting you to buy into themes and actions that you had never really thought much about. The science of a thin, hot atmosphere on a bleak world was just clever sets and dialog, but it factored into the plot without any CGI. You would make the intuitive leap unwittingly that early life there was harsh and brutal. Normally as a kid you would think that meant an analogue to Native American or Bedouin culture, but *Star Trek* changed your course heading seamlessly. The Vulcans were not human, and their culture did not quite fit. It was a tightly controlled existence with very little individual wiggle room. When T'Pau said "The air is the air; what can be done?" you might have seen the subtle glimpse in her delivery that she thought it was a bad situation Kirk and Spock were in. She knew McCoy might have a trick up his sleeve and the doctor didn't disappoint. By sticking to her ways but being open to universal concepts like friendship and well-played deception she could get everyone out of this with no one dying. That's a highly logical being. You can see why everyone held her in such a high regard.

I tried to copy the Vulcan hand salute and to my surprise it came quite naturally. It marked me as a true fan and a person of great finger dexterity. No one I met knew what it meant when I used it, but I always took the greeting as the best way to make a new friendship. Many years later when introduced to my future wife her returning it made me realize I was not alone. Marriage on Vulcan seemed complicated and serious, much like here, but with slightly less mortal combat. We were married in Cleveland though; Vulcan was too far, and we didn't want a destination wedding.

Kind and Christian values were big in my little starship home as a kid. On *Star Trek* I got to see how they worked in the world, when they didn't, and what to do then. Learning tolerance and kindness was as simple as the Federation's "How can we help?" attitude. Many times, that made a difficult situation easier to understand. Science would work it out, or Medical would have the answer, or Engineering would fix what was wrong.

However, here in the real world was always something that couldn't be repaired or fixed or overcome. Wars happen, people get sick and die, sometimes the bad guys win. That was a tough lesson for me to learn and it wasn't until much later as an adult I came to accept that. It made me a lesser person in my eyes to accept the existence of the no win scenario. I never could see the forest for the trees when it came to success versus failure. But James T. Kirk never quit, so neither did I.

Kirk would probably be my favorite character growing up. You could see the kid in him peek out sometimes and the humor he used to deal with stressful situations was inspiring. You could just tell that serving under him as captain would be a unique experience. He was loyal to the crew and its ideals, loyal to his friends and not afraid to admit when he was wrong or foolish. He drove his crew when they needed a push, and he expected them to be excellent. You can see this also fed into his fierce determination regarding them as well. When one of his crew died, he knew their names and it was not just the price of doing business on the frontier. He wanted who was responsible and knew that would also allow his crew to see him lead by example.

They would stick together and take care of each other, like a little family in Ohio.

Jeff "Venture" Fournier is a non-fiction and multi-genre pulp writer. Jeff has primarily been published with Airship 27 with Sword and Sorcery ("Sinbad and the Isle of Madness" in their Sinbad series anthology) and the creation of the Printer's Devil (in the 1930's mystery man type) for Airship's New Pulp Anthology. He is also a reviewer that has been published in several print and E-magazines for outdoors and gear reviews. In his spare times he likes wood crafting and exploring the universe.

BOB'S PERSONAL LOG

BY ROBERT GREENBERGER

I've often referenced this pivotal moment but let me tell it again. I used to go to bed with my radio tuned to WNBC, listening to talk host Brad Crandall, and drifting to sleep. For whatever reason, one night, I came downstairs. I didn't normally get up for water, so maybe I actually tried to dial in. I don't recall. What stuck in my mind, though, was looking from the kitchen into the playroom (as we called it), and there was my father watching something on our recently acquired color television.

There were people in colorful shirts stepping onto a platform, and then they vanished.

Now, I had been reading comic books at a voracious clip for a few years by then, and was watching kids' SF on WPIX and WNEW, shows ranging from *The Adventures of Superman* reruns to Gerry Anderson's wonderful Supermarionation output. But this was live-action, in color, and they vanished!

The 1960s was a formative time for America, with the arrival of JFK, the Beatles, man on the Moon, etc. It also introduced controversial matters such as the Pill and the Vietnam War. As a kid not yet in double digits for most of this period, all that was background noise to the colorful antics of larger-than-life heroes. It began with a Superman comic book in 1964, and like Dorothy first gazing at Oz, it was revelatory. One comic led to many, and then Superman on TV led to finding similar action/adventure shows, mostly cartoons and puppets, but they stirred the imagination. Of course, things were notched up a level on January 12, 1966, and the first airing of *Batman*, but those are essays for another trilogy of books (all available from Jim Beard and Crazy 8 Press, naturally).

My parents bought a low, wide table where I would sit in the playroom, front, and center near the television, and I would play with toys or, more often than not, try to draw my own comics.

Let's just say I was primed for the shifts in popular culture, from the ubiquitous Westerns to espionage and action shows.

I didn't see what that was about again until August 30, 1968. I was ten, and my parents let me stay up a wee bit later during the summer. I was spinning the dial looking for something during the summer rerun season and came upon something that stirred my mind. I distinctly recall catching "A Piece of the Action" on the black and white TV in the room I shared with my brother. Now it had a name: *Star Trek*.

With the funny lines and somewhat familiar gangsters, it was a great introduction to the 23rd Century, so yeah, I was hooked.

I am sure I saw some bits and pieces between the summer and April 1969, but I have no recollection. Instead, I distinctly recall the Bookmobile pulling into the front parking circle in front of Cantiague Elementary School, and as my sixth-grade class entered the narrow confines, stocked with paperbacks of all sorts on wire racks, there was *Star Trek 3* just released by Bantam Books. I bought it, then sought out the previous two volumes elsewhere.

I was transported and fell in love with this series and its dashing crew.

At Floyd's, a local department store, I came across *The Making of Star Trek* that summer and instantly bought it. Here was a book that revealed all the secrets of television production, and I was enraptured. Now I knew how Robert April became James T. Kirk and more information that I devoured.

And then came Wednesday, September 10, 1969. WPIX, then my favorite television station, began rerunning *Star Trek*. The final NBC rerun was August 19, and then the 79 episodes were sold into syndication, and I could finally see it all. The series first ran at 6:30 p.m. (following *Batman* which arrived in syndication the year before), and my mom would serve me, my brother, and my sister in the kitchen, slightly raised from the family room, and we could watch over the railing.

To say I was enraptured is a mild way of describing it. This show had action, drama, humor, aliens, sexy women (I was beginning to notice them)—everything! In time, I acquired a small cassette tape recorder and knew the shows by heart so I could capture my favorite music cues and lines of dialogue for a personal mixtape that would keep me company for a while.

I was buying the novelizations as they arrived, somehow missed the initial Gold Key comics, and discovered I wasn't the only kid hooked. Sometime during junior high, as memory serves, my friend James Johneas and Stuart Weiss mounted a home movie version and converted James' basement into cardboard sets. Because I could do Scotty's burr and owned a red shirt, I got that role, glasses included.

So, yeah, I was sorta, kinda an original Trekkie, although I didn't discover the zines until much later.

But I was so deep into my love affair with the series that I was able to attend the first *Star Trek* Convention in New York City on January 12, 1972. By then, my best friend Jeff Strell and I were making regular Long Island Railroad treks to NYC's Penn Station, crossing the street to the Statler Hilton Hotel, and attending comic cons. We attended one day, I think it was Saturday, and it was a mob, unlike the busy but passable comic cons. That said, we did marvel at the NASA displays, complete with space suits. And there was Isaac Asimov, whose *Asimov's Mysteries* was the first non-media-tie-in SF book I read. He was standing there and chatting with people. Crazy!

We packed into a ballroom, and from a distance, I could see Gene Roddenberry address the crowds before showing an episode (nope, couldn't tell you which one) and, if I recall, the infamous Blooper Reel.

A convention dedicated to a television series was unheard of, and as with the incredible syndicated ratings, *Star Trek* was suddenly the talk of the town. Even in 1972, there were discussions over a revival, although we got the *Animated Series* instead that fall.

I read Blish's *Spock Must Die!* and Western's *Mission to Horatius* by Mack Reynolds, the first original novels, with more to come over the next decade, cementing my interest in *Star Trek* in all forms.

Interestingly, it was a vastly different connection with *Star Trek* than it was with comic books, which took primary place in my affections. For whatever reason, I wanted *in* on the *Trek* action in a different way than comics. So, when I saw that the con was coming back in 1973 and looking for volunteers, I contacted them. I was a gopher, stationed wherever I was needed, and did whatever was asked of me. It was glorious, allowing me to get close to the action and still see the celebrity panels.

That second con was when Leonard Nimoy, in town for something else, decided to stop by and see what the fuss was all about. I was among those taken into confidence and was part of the flying-V security detail (as was fellow Crazy 8er Paul Kupperberg) that allowed Nimoy to stroll from the entrance into the ballroom to rapturous applause.

I performed the same function in 1974 and 1975. The events blur with time, but highlights include using replica Vulcan weapons to guard a side door to the dealers' room, which had two effects. One, it caught the attention of a photographer from a New Jersey newspaper, and second, I tried to prevent Walter Koenig from using the forbidden doorway, earning me a nasty look (in my defense, he was moving so fast, I didn't notice who it was; thankfully, he doesn't hold it against me). I snagged an interview with George Takei for my high school paper which began a casual friendship that endures. There was the time programming had a hole for some reason (likely George being late), and I sat with some volunteers, helping David Gerrold lead a filk singalong using a lyric sheet provided to every attendee (still have mine).

Being a volunteer, and a veteran with each passing year, I was granted access to the massive suite that the guests used to chill between appearances. There was the chance for fun one-on-ones with the guests and being on hand for a group serenade of "Battle Hymn of the 1975 ST Con", sung to Majel and Gene Roddenberry at the end of one show, when he dubbed us all crazy.

In 1975, Roddenberry was in the con suite and made it known he wanted some lemon wedges for his cocktail. They were out, so whoever was running the suite handed me some cash and explained

I needed to go into Grand Central Station, beneath the Commodore Hotel where we were, to find a grocer with lemons. Now, I had never been in the bowels of Grand Central, the venerable transit hub which opened in 1913. As described on its eponymous 1937-1954 radio program, it was "the crossroads of a million private lives, a gigantic stage on which are played a thousand dramas daily." My personal drama had me enter the place and be nearly crushed by the Friday night rush hour commuters racing to make their connections. Grand Central has two levels, and I descended deeper in search of the elusive yellow fruit. I felt lost and admittedly bewildered. Finally, to my right was the equivalent of today's mini-mart, and by the doorway was a basket with lemons and limes. I made my purchase and managed to find my way back to the surface world and then the suite where a grateful Roddenberry awaited. (I had an on-and-off relationship with the man, chatting him up at cons, pushing him in his wheelchair when he spoke at SUNY-Binghamton, where I was a student, and finally, on the receiving end of excoriating memos in his name when he regained input on licensed material as part of his *Next Generation* deal.)

In 1976, the original con committee held its final show, but a wicked flu ran through the staff. Claire Eddy (now of Tor Books) and Steve Whitfield (the first man to ever kiss me on the lips—imagine my surprise) ran the helpers, who were zombies trying to keep things from falling apart. Rosemary Krist stepped up and ran things. For whatever reason, that brought me even closer to the running of a con, always where Rosemary needed me, the closest I would ever come.

It was also a transitional year. I was a high school senior, intent on being a writer. I had already written my first zine article, "It's the Clerks Who Run the Government," a celebration of the Bridge's crew, for *-273°C*. For their next issue, I doubled as a con reporter, grabbing pictures of the 1976 guests, including first-timer Howard Weinstein, who had written the animated "The Pirates of Orion." We struck up a conversation as I took his picture by the elevators, which has led to a friendship to this day.

In the late spring, the con held a thank you party to one and all, and there, Rosemary and I sparked. This led to an invitation to spend a weekend with this older woman (by seven years), and childhood ended.

Star Trek fueled my imagination and provided countless experiences and memories. It provided me fodder for stories beginning with my junior high school paper right up through my time at *Starlog*. I made friends through those five years of NY cons, connections that remain in place today. I went from being a con attendee and volunteer to being a guest at *Star Trek* conventions. And then came the chance to produce original *Trek* stories as I took the helm of DC Comics' *Star Trek* comic, steering it for eight years. And that opportunity led to my writing *Trek* fiction.

There's no knowing what influences from childhood would prove pivotal in shaping a life and a career. When I was ten, *Star Trek* was just cool and fun to watch. Now, it's woven so tightly into the fiber of my being that I cannot see myself without that optimistic view of the future as being a part of who I am.

Robert Greenberger has had a career including positions at Starlog Press, DC Comics, Gist Communications, Marvel Comics, *Weekly World News*, Famous Monsters of Filmland, and ComicMix. As a writer, his credits range from fiction to nonfiction and media tie-ins to original works. A cofounder of Crazy 8 Press, he continues to write an edit. He's also a High School English teacher in Maryland, where he makes his home with his wife Deb and their dog Harley. For more, see www.bobgreenberger.com.

GROWING UP IN THAT FORGOTTEN SPACE SECTOR: THE FINGER LAKES

BY ED CATTO

Back then, watching *Star Trek* was like watching a sunset. Every night you'd wait and watch; it had the potential to be awesome. Even when it wasn't spectacular it was still impressive.

Like every sunset, you could plan your schedule around it. In fact, each day you knew when it would occur. But we weren't in control. The times to enjoy *Star Trek*, the "real" *Star Trek* television show, were dictated to us.

And like a sunset, it would be over all too soon. That's the way we felt about *Star Trek* in those days. Oh sure, there was *hope* that there would be more, but that seemed like a pipe dream. There was *hope* that I'd someday date Cheryl Tiegs too, but I kind of knew that too was unrealistic.

License to Trek

Growing up an Italian American, family was very important to me. Let's get real here. "They" just made me type that. In actuality, I think that *food* was important to us. Every Sunday my grandma and grandpa would orchestrate a sprawling Sunday Dinner. Although it was called "dinner," it was more of a Sunday Lunch. The whole family would come over and we'd enjoy all the greatest hits from every Italian restaurant's menu.

Just like every Italian kid, I need to brag that my grandmother was an outstanding cook. She even supplied meatballs to several local restaurants. We never wanted to miss this weekly event.

After the traditional cannoli at Grandma's, my dad would reward my brother Colin and I with a trip to a small local convenience store, although we never called them convenience stores back then. It was called Pauline's Newsstand, and this will be shocker to you, but another one of our Italian relatives owned and operated it. Both my brother and I were allowed to buy one thing each Sunday at the store.

This is how I started my life-long fascination with comics. It was all from choosing one comic per Sunday from the spinner rack in the back of Pauline's. When I usually tell this story, I talk about how my brother Colin missed out because he would squander this once-a-week gift by selecting some cheap toy. You might remember a few of these cheap toys that were sold back then: balsa wood airplanes or paddles with rubber balls attached by an elastic or even goofy sunglasses.

What a waste!

Except…when it wasn't. There was a time when he proved to be wiser and cleverer than I was. It was when Colin selected the *Star Trek* plastic pistol as his "one item" from Pauline's on that fateful Sunday.

What an amazing toy! *Star Trek* was "over," or about to be over, at this point. Like a car with an empty gas tank that's still running on fumes, merchandise like this plastic pistol was one way we helped the show live on. This off-product toy was curious on so many levels. It didn't look like any of the props used on the show. It certainly wasn't a phaser. Instead, it just propelled little plastic flat circles, called Jet Disks, with a (I guess) futuristic design. The packaging didn't even look *Star Trek*-y. Not to young experts like us, anyways. But it plainly stated—right there on the package—that this was a *Star Trek* gun. Painted faces of Spock and Kirk were there too, so it *had* to be legitimate.

We'd often play backyard games like Army. If any of the neighborhood kids didn't have a toy gun, a simple stick would do just fine. We weren't picky. But this pistol. Wow! This would be a game changer when we played *Star Trek*.

On the other hand, I don't think we played *Star Trek* that much. After all, one kid could be Captain Kirk, one kid could be Spock, but everyone else would be relegated to portray the less interesting Enterprise crew. After all, who really wanted to be Sulu or a red-shirted security guard? Even then, we knew what would happen to those guys.

Danger, Will Robinson

Back in the ancient days when every home had just "one screen," you had to be judicious and diplomatic when deciding what to watch. Growing up, we were a one-television house. Hard to imagine today when every kid relaxes with multiple screens.

My brother and I worked hard to elevate our art of sibling fighting to an expert level. We could each have earned our PhD in "Brother-Fighting" before puberty.

One of the ten zillion things we argued about was what to watch on TV. Usually we'd navigate to compromise, as (1) we liked many of the same things and (2) one of us would bash the other's brains in and triumphantly, albeit briefly, control the television.

There were times when this was an especially sticky wicket. WNEW (Channel 5 in New York City but broadcast, paradoxically, on Channel 4 upstate) ran *Lost in Space* episodes at same time WPIX (NYC's Channel 11) broadcast *Star Trek* reruns. Now, there's a lot to love about *Lost in Space*. Highest on that list, to my young mind at the time, was Professor's Robinson's gorgeous daughter, Judy Robinson.

(Years later, I would share a moment with actor Mark Goddard, who played Judy Robinson's boyfriend, Don West, on the show. He wistfully mused, "She sure was a beauty.")

But I was unwilling to concede to my brother that he could ever be right. To me, there was *no* situation where watching an episode of *Lost In Space* was a better idea than watching an episode of *Star Trek*. Even if it was the Space Hippies episode.

My father, who had by this time developed a modern-day Wisdom of Solomon in order to get through each day with his combative sons, came up with a unique solution that became a permanent family policy. In cases where the two brothers were unable to resolve their television conflicts, I would be granted the authority to choose the channel and Colin would be granted the authority to either turn the TV on or off.

Looking back, it *was* pretty brilliant.

Reading is Fandomental

We knew that *Star Trek* was "a real thing" when we stumbled across the *Star Trek Mission to Horatius* hardcover. This was published by Whitman. To us, as pop culture kids, when a property was published by Whitman, it was a sign of the highest quality. After all, there were also books from Whitman focused on *Zorro* and the *Green Hornet*.

It turns out that *Mission to Horatius* was in fact the very first *Star Trek* original novel.

The story may not have been absolutely dreadful, but it was totally forgettable. Little additions, like Sulu's pet rat, seemed a bit off to a young fan. Starved for more *Star Trek* adventures, we took those curious little things in stride.

The illustrations in *Mission to Horatius* were provided by Mack Reynolds. These line drawings seemed a little rough as Reynolds employed a jagged line. I probably couldn't articulate it at the time, but that style worked against the smooth sleekness of the series. While the show looked elegant and futuristic, Reynold's art seemed better suited to a war story or an outdoorsy little-boy-and-his-dog adventure.

And when you add in the fact that the endpapers showcased the Starship *Enterprise* with jet streams trailing from the nacelles…well, we just rolled our eyes in that "stupid adults!" way that smart children always have done and always will do.

Adults Getting It Wrong

The comics were the same way. It would take a while for comics to get *Star Trek* right. In the late 60s and early 70s, there were enough super hero comics to overwhelm and inundate a kid like me. There were a lot of other comics that looked interesting to me, but there just wasn't enough time, resources and energy to enjoy every comic that was published.

We'd all revisit that idea in our forties and fifties chasing nostalgia through back issues.

So once in a while we'd read Gold Key comics. They were, for whatever reason, a barber shop staple in my hometown. I remember trying to understand how they could photograph *Man of The Atom* (spoiler alert: they were really paintings) for the covers yet serve up drab interior artwork for the stories.

As a kid, the Gold Key *Star Trek* comics were extra-perplexing. The photo covers (with *real* photos), featuring Captain Kirk or Mr. Spock, signaled a sense of veracity and authenticity, but as soon as we started reading comic stories within, we were shocked.

How could the adults who presumably created these comics be so wrong about everything?

The *Enterprise* didn't have jet streams coming out of the nacelles. Spock never said things like "Great Comets!" and the Enterprise crew never behaved like a bunch of non-union deep-sea divers. Didn't these grown-ups even watch the show?

Well, it turns out that often they did not! At least early on. The early ones were produced by Italian creators with little familiarity with the show, working from scripts. But like the Whitman book, we'd soldier on through these peculiar oddities and smile thinking, "At least we have *some* Kirk and Spock adventures!"

Beyond The Farthest Star, *i.e.*, our Trips to the "Big City" Mall

I grew up in a small town (with a big history), and we revered the library. Each week, my mom would take me and my brother there.

She had a great routine – she'd check out a stack of books, usually mysteries or thrillers, and then find the one or two she really liked and read them. I admired how when the entire family gathered to watch TV (does any family even do that anymore?), she would pull out her book and read a few chapters undistracted by the television set.

But the implicit message to me and my brothers, Colin, and younger brother Chris who was on the scene by now, was: it's good to read. And secondarily, it's good to read a lot. She'd always have the current book she was reading on the kitchen table or the coffee table. There was no doom-scrolling in those days, she would just pick up her book and read a couple of chapters.

The local library was wonderful (it still is, in fact), but in those days they didn't keep up with trendy or pop literature. Oh sure, they had Bradbury and Asimov novels available, but there were no *Star Trek* novels to check out back then.

But every once in a while, Mom would take us to the "big city" mall. Fairmount Fair was a glorious place. Imagine: an enclosed mini city filled with stores! And there were even lamp posts inside the mall. Stores dedicated to just one thing—like toys or teen fashions. Absurdly, capitalistically, brilliant!

The Kay-Bee Toys store in this mall was really something. For a while my brother and I were collecting Corgi cars and we couldn't wait to visit Kay Bee. We even created the Save-Up Club, so the neighborhood chums could all pool our resources. Sounds a bit socialistic by today's standards, I will admit. I'll save *that* story for the Corgi Collections anthology.

The other best-store-ever in the mall, which seemed like a magical place akin to Oz or Narnia, was the bookstore. Imagine—a store that only sold books. And calendars too if you wanted to split hairs. And it wasn't only all those stuffy books written by ancient scribes like Dickens and Hemingway. It had all these books with our favorites from the world of entertainment. Brand names like Disney and Superman.

(Don't worry—I'd learn to appreciate those guys and went on a major Hemingway bender years later.)

The Science Fiction section of this store—the library didn't really have that back then—had these incredible paperback books adapting *Star Trek* episodes. What an incredible idea! This series of short stories would collect the novelizations of a few episodes, and then combine them together in a series simplistically denoted as *Star Trek 4*, or *Star Trek 5*.

TOS television episodes were so fleeting to us back then. We had no way to record or replay episodes at our discretion. Every time a network or cable station showed us an episode of something we loved, we were surprised and grateful.

Oh sure, sometimes *TV Guide* would give a summary of the episode to be shown, and you could figure out if that was a "good one" or not, but most times you would just sit in front of the TV and see what they served up.

These Bantam Books written (primarily) by science fiction writer James Blish were more than just books. They were more than just novelizations. In those halcyon days of yesteryear, before streaming shows, before Blu-ray discs, before DVDs and VHS tapes, before even scripts pirated from the internet—these books were a way for Trek fans to enjoy episodes on their own terms and on their own schedule.

They were glorious. We all knew the actor's voices. We knew all the sound effects, from the phaser's blast to the pneumatic swoosh of the Enterprise's doors. We all knew the theme song music. We all knew the various musical interludes, even if we didn't know how they were meant to be used. We would mentally sprinkle any of the series' signature elements into these novelizations wherever we wanted.

As fandom got more and more sophisticated, fans began to notice incongruities and inconsistencies between the original episodes and Blish's adaptations. But we weren't anywhere close to that yet. Back then, these paperbacks were like the tablets handed from above, almost directly from the Great Bird directly to fans.

Likewise, *The Making of Star Trek*, by Stephen E. Whitfield and Gene Rodenberry, and *The World of Star Trek*, by David Gerrold were also like little *Star Trek* bibles.

The *Star Trek* Blueprint for Partying in High School

We all talk about how prescient *Star Trek* was, or innovative, or how groundbreaking, but *Star Trek* was also about friendships. If it was only an adventure story about three guys on a rocket ship, I imagine it would have been very mundane. But the simple premise of a guy and his two closest friends, often advising him based on two very different worldviews, was a thread woven through the fabric of the show.

My local friends weren't doctors or Vulcans, but we too were excited to share adventures together. And we'd often pre-game with the shared experience of watching *Star Trek*.

Attending high school in the late 70s and early 80s, our weekends often fell into a certain pattern. On Saturday Nights, my little group would furiously work to uncover the best parties…or the best avenue for maximum mischief. We'd call each other on the phone, coordinate and build a consensus one-by-one in those pre-group chat days.

One pal in particular, Pete Hoffmann, was also a *Trek* fan. And wouldn't you know it, but those frantic and furious calls would typically take place early on Saturday nights. *Star Trek* was on WPIX at 6:00 pm, so I would usually work to delay my planning conversations until it was over.

When our little collection of reprobates gathered, Pete and I would typically begin our weekend with a conversation about the episode that just aired.

"Didja See it?"

"I can't believe that they did that."

"Code Two, Lieutenant!"

Our non-*Trek* pals never quite understood it. But then again, when they babbled on about the recent Mets game, I had trouble getting any enthusiasm about that too.

But those episodes were, in many ways, our blueprint for every Saturday Night of our High School years. It was a simple plan: Open yourself up for a new adventure, on adventures, outwit our enemies, find an exotic beauty (maybe even kiss her), accomplish something extraordinary and unexpected with your pals, and then neatly wrap it all up at the end.

And, of course, implicit in the formula was the notion of getting ready to do it all again next Saturday.

This was important because back then, our understanding was that *Star Trek* was fleeting. We all knew it was only on for three seasons, and we weren't ever getting any more. And we knew we had to be attentive to the broadcasters' schedules, because we, as individuals, could never dictate the exact time to watch an episode. We were at the mercy of the television timetable. How quickly that all changed.

Memories and Lessons Learned

Star Trek offered a lot of lessons to be learned by impressionable young TV generation children. Use your wits in tough spots. Don't kill bad guys, even if they are big mean lizards. Rely on your friends. Have a trick or two up your sleeve, and it's ok to fib a bit in these situations. Leave any bigotry in your room as there's no room for it amongst smart people. Break the rules when it's the right thing to do. When you're trying to do great things, risk is your business. And that the words of the Constitution were not written for the chiefs or kings, or the warriors, or the rich, or the powerful -- but for all the people! They must apply to everyone, or they mean nothing. And every episode taught us to approach challenges with a smile and a bit of a swagger.

Seems to me, those were pretty good lessons. And I treasure all those *Star Trek* memories too.

Although he still feels he's just one step away from filling out that application for Star Fleet, **Ed Catto** keeps busy reading, teaching and writing about comics, and pop-culture for *Pop Culture Squad* (in his long-running *With Further Ado* column), *Back Issue Magazine*,

The Overstreet Comic Book Price Guide, *The 13th Dimension* and *Comic Mix*. As an artist, his work reflects the influence of and appreciation for the great comic and pulp illustrators. Employing traditional techniques, he was twice voted "Best Interior Artist" for the annual Pulp Factory Awards. Having recently returned to the Finger Lakes area, Ed has joined the faculty of Ithaca College's School of Business and founded Agendae, a strategic marketing firm. Between teaching, consulting, drawing, and writing, Ed tirelessly continues to whittle down the teetering tower of books on his nightstand.

GIANT-SIZE TREK THING

BY RICH HANDLEY

"Hey, don't change the channel! I'm watching *Star Trek!*"

"It's my turn! I wanna watch *Good Times!*"

"*Good Times* is stupid. It's just that doofus Jimmie Walker yelling 'Dy-no-mite!' *Star Trek* is much better."

"*Star Trek* is stupid. It's just a plastic spaceship and fake pointed ears. At least *Good Times* could actually happen."

"You're stupid! And I'm watching *Star Trek.*"

"No, *you're* stupid! I'm telling Mom—"

"Alright, TV off. Both of you go to your rooms, *now!*"

"But that's not fair! *Star Trek* is on! I was watching first!"

"I wanna watch *Good Tiiimes!*"

"*Star Trek! Star Trek!*"

"No! *Good Times!!*"

Sigh. Welcome to my childhood.

I was born in 1968, during the summer hiatus between the final episode of *Star Trek*'s second season, "Assignment: Earth," and Season Three's dubious opener, "Spock's Brain." My mother Joni, a first-generation fan, had shared with me her love of not only *Star Trek*, but also *Planet of the Apes*, *The Twilight Zone*, *The Outer Limits*, and more. She was a very socially conscious person, so the messages of these stories greatly appealed to her, and she instilled their values in me. My sister Jody—my costar in the above recreation—has no interest in science fiction but is just as socially conscious.

Our *Star Trek* vs. *Good Times* debate was fairly frequent in 1980, since we only had a single television and the two shows aired at the same time. But it's interesting to me that much like *Star Trek*, *Good Times*, a U.S. sitcom about a financially struggling African American family in inner-city Chicago (which was *not* stupid, I know—well, not before the silly hijinks of Walker's J.J. Evans took center stage, at least), dealt with topical issues in a sophisticated manner. Jody and I developed vastly different interests, yet my mother's worldview and activism had influenced us both.

The series ended a month shy of my first birthday, so I'd be lying if I claimed to have any memories of watching it during its initial airing. When I was a baby, though, my family lived in a compact apartment, with my playpen kept in the living room. So, although I couldn't follow what was happening on the screen, I can truthfully say I was there for the final season, since my mom watched the series in that same room. While she enjoyed each new voyage of the starship *Enterprise*, I drooled on my onesie, soiled my diaper, and otherwise embraced every complex nuance of the infant experience.

Still, I was *there*, man. I can look you straight in the eye and stake my claim as a fellow first-gen Trekkie, even if only on an extreme technicality. Well, sort of. A little. If you squint and tilt your head. OK, probably not at all, since I had no idea *Star Trek* even existed at the time and was likely focused more on figuring out how to get my tiny foot into my tiny mouth. But the judges will allow it because the judges are me. Thankfully, I didn't stay a baby forever, so that extreme technicality was replaced by an extreme *Trek* mentality, thanks to syndicated reruns.

As a child with a single-digit age during the era that gave us *The Rockford Files*, *Young Frankenstein*, and Marvel Comics' chuckle-inducing *Giant-Size Man Thing*, I fell in love with *Star Trek* not for the aspects that appeal to me now. I freely admit the show's greatest appeal largely escaped me when I was seven years old. So, it wasn't the topical commentary regarding 20th-century societal problems that kept me watching in the beginning, nor was it the compelling mix of Shakespearean themes with World War II and Cold War motifs, wrapped up in clever science-fiction trappings so network censors would overlook the scathing mirror being held up to racism, fascism, capitalism, warmongering, religious dogmatism, and other evils.

It also wasn't the savvy juxtaposition of comedy and tragedy, nor the pitch-perfect pairing of William Shatner's over-the-top thespianism with Leonard Nimoy's coolly calculated persona and De-

Forest Kelley's crotchety Southern gentlemen demeanor. Nope, my appreciation for all that came later. At age seven, you see, I simply thought the hissing lizard man and the giant rock creature and the giant green space-hand and the giant black cat and the acid-spewing meatball pizza monster were cool.

For this then-budding sci-fi geek, "the more giants, the better" was how I viewed the world, which explains why I also loved *Land of the Giants, Land of the Lost, Lost in Space,* and Godzilla movies. Also, I got a kick out of hearing Spock call everything "illogical" (my mom drilled into my head that it was *Mister* Spock, not *Doctor* Spock—he was a science officer, not a pediatrician). Oh, and the phasers made neat "pew pew" sounds. Never underestimate the appeal of "pew pew" phaser sounds to a preadolescent, particularly when there are also "eeeeeeezzzhhhhhh" transporter sounds and "ssshhhhhhwhaa!" automatic door-opening sounds.

I grew up in New York's Hudson Valley, spent my preteen years in North Carolina (where the *Good Times* scenario played out), and then returned to New York at age thirteen, where I've remained ever since. I no longer recall what station aired *Star Trek* in the South, but here in New York it was WPIX, which broadcast my favorite show daily as part of a late-night block that also included *The Honeymooners, The Odd Couple,* and *The Twilight Zone.* Even though I had school the next day, I of course *had* to stay up and watch them all. I could always sleep during social studies.

Three of those four shows have aged relatively well, by the way, despite their somewhat outdated attitudes. The other is *The Honeymooners.* (Woah, there! Don't grab your pitchforks just yet, Kramden fans! *The Honeymooners* is still funny, but viewed through a modern-day lens, it's not so easy to overlook Ralph's tendency to constantly threaten his wife with bang-zoom-moon violence.)

As an adult, I've spent a great deal of time writing about fictional universes, dissecting them from every conceivable angle. That probably came as no surprise to my parents, given how fully I had immersed myself in *Trek* lore starting at age eleven. My mom and I had watched every classic episode countless times and we knew them well, so when the beautiful and underrated cinematic brilliance that is *Star Trek: The Motion Picture* debuted in 1979, we of course went to the theater to watch it—twice.

If you're noticing a gap, that's because even though I'd been a child when *Star Trek: The Animated Series* aired in the 1970s, I missed out on watching it until the late '80s, first because I'd been unaware of it, and later because it wasn't available for viewing once I'd learned it existed. When it reran in my area, I meticulously recorded the episodes on grainy VHS tapes. Luckily, they didn't air opposite *Good Times* (or else blood might have been spilled), though I may have had to coerce my other sisters, Susan and Julie, to stop rewatching *North and South* long enough for me to record each day's episode.

Our little brother Eric, thirteen years my junior, loved the *Star Trek* cartoon, despite not otherwise giving a hoot about the franchise. He was more a *Teenage Mutant Ninja Turtles* kind of kid. As for me, I was skeptical about watching it the first time, for the idea of the Sixties' *Star Trek* revived as a children's cartoon seemed… wrong somehow. I quickly realized, however, that the only thing wrong had been my own prejudgment. Had I learned *nothing* from what Spock had taught about embracing infinite diversity in infinite combinations?

Despite some goofy bits, such as a giant Spock and giant tribbles (I was no longer that giant-enamored seven-year-old), the show was an impressive achievement. If you ignore the animation quirks of that era, such as the frequent footage reuse, the silly way the characters ran, and the over-abundance of the color pink, *The Animated Series* was a worthy continuation of the 1960s show. I view them as one combined series, and I'll die on that space-hill, shortsighted 1990s Paramount edict be damned. But I digress, as Peter David would say. We now return to our discussion of *The Motion Picture*.

Reactions to the film were somewhat lukewarm, but my mom and I vehemently disagreed with reviewers. *Star Trek* was back, baby! Sure, the pensive pacing earned it harsh nicknames like *The Motionless Picture*, but as far as we were concerned, it was riveting, albeit a rehash of (and improvement on) the episode "The Changeling." The movie didn't just propel the franchise back into the spotlight, though. It ushered in a bounty of licensed publications, both fiction and non-fiction, based around the classic show and the newly launched theatrical revival.

My allowance was pretty meager back in the day, even by 1980 standards, and I tended to use it to buy lots of baseball cards...which, looking back, is inexplicable since I've *never* been a fan of baseball (not even the Giants). Still, when I came across a trio of *Trek* titles at our local Waldenbooks, I *had* to have them. *The Official Star Trek Trivia Book* was credited to "Trivia Master Rafe Needleman (Organian)," which made me smile. The *Star Trek Spaceflight Chronology*, from Stanley and Fred Goldstein and Rick Sternbach, would inspire me to write similar books decades later. And David A. Kimble's *Star Trek: The Motion Picture Blueprints* were a thing of beauty.

Something changed in that moment. I'd never felt the need before to amass TV show tie-in books. Lunchboxes? Yes. Posters and toys? Sure. Cheaply printed iron-on T-shirts and jean patches that faded and flaked off after only a few washings? Hey, I was a child of the Seventies. A *Planet of the Apes* garbage can? Life would have been meaningless without it. But tie-in books? Not so much, which is ironic since my shelves these days are filled to the brim with them.

That wasn't the case in 1980. My reading habits at that time primarily involved young crime-solvers like the Hardy Boys, Nancy Drew, Encyclopedia Brown, and the Bobbsey Twins. I couldn't get enough of clever kid-sleuths, and I had shelves full of their adventures that had once belonged to my father Vinnie. Books about TV characters? Not really, no—not even the clever young crime-solving kid-sleuths of *Scooby-Doo*, which I watched all the time.

Don't get me wrong, I would *read* tie-in books if a friend or cousin had some, or if I saw one at a library. I was, after all, a kid. I just had no great urge to *own* them—that is, until the Waldenbooks visit. Those books and blueprints were *cool*, and they called to me like dog treats call to Scooby-Doo and Shaggy Rogers. Like a plate of mushies calls to Boxey and Muffet. Like a bag of finely cooked meth calls to Skinny Pete and Badger. Like a—okay, fine, you get the point.

Embarrassing memory alert: I didn't have enough allowance saved up to buy those items, so I asked my mom to purchase them for me, promising to pay her back. For some reason, I was adamant that I had to get them *that day*, as though the publisher or store would pulp all remaining copies the moment we left, making it impossible to find them again. My mom declined, so I…er…kind of had a hissy fit in the store.

I'm not proud of that moment. I was nearly twelve years old and should have known better. But it happened, and so I left empty-handed. I complained all the way home, while my mom drove the station wagon in silent fury. Later that night, she handed me all three publications in a huff. It seems she'd picked them up as a birthday gift when I hadn't been looking, but because I had acted like such a petulant brat, she no longer cared about my birthday, so I might as well just have the damn things now. Ouch. Did I mention that my mom had mastered the art of Jewish guilt?

The thing about child guilt, though, is that it doesn't last long. So, yeah, I sat there feeling awkward and shamed by her angry generosity, but a few minutes later I shrugged it off and started reading, 'cause now I had the books I'd wanted! My preteen immaturity forgotten, I poured through the stylistic *Spaceflight Chronology*, gazed at the detailed floor-by-floor blueprints, and tested how smart I was with trivia questions. The trivia book contained an episode guide, so I began (oh, god, the collector in me cringes at this) checking off each episode *with a magic marker* (oh, the pain!) to make sure I had, in fact, seen them all.

When I collect something, I commit to it. Now that I had a *Star Trek* trivia book, it was imperative I be able to correctly answer every single question, proving I, too, was an Organian like Rafe Needleman. Now that I had blueprints, I had no choice but to memorize the starship's layouts in all their two-dimensional glory. Now that I had a chronology chronicling centuries of historical events, it was my duty to reread it until I knew everything that had happened from *Sputnik* to Starfleet. Anything less would have been uncivilized.

She couldn't have known it at the time, of course, but in buying me those books and blueprints, my mother had not just gotten me an early birthday present. She hadn't merely picked up merchandise based on a franchise we'd enjoyed together. And she hadn't succeeded solely in guilting the heck out of me by rewarding public misbehavior with undeserved prizes. No, she'd done something far greater that day: she'd set me on a decades-long journey into fandom, and thus on a career path.

A few years later, using the trivia book as my guide, I began taking detailed notes about each episode I watched, then typing it up on an old-style typewriter in black and red ink, determined to sear it all into my memory. Even when I stayed overnight at my friend Danny's house, I still watched *Trek* at midnight and jotted down notes, more than a little self-conscious about the amused expression on his father's face. It was this that secured in me a love of crafting words into narratives.

Once I was old enough to earn spending money, I picked up Bjo Trimble's *Star Trek Concordance* and *On the Good Ship Enterprise*, then started on the licensed novels and comics, culminating in my wallpapering my bedroom (and later my college dorm room) with *Star Trek* posters, much to my stepmom Carol's bemusement. I recorded every episode on homemade VHS tapes, then collected the official mail-order sets from Columbia House Video and discovered to my delight that the WPIX versions had been heavily edited to allow for commercials. Those Columbia House videos were revelatory, for as they arrived in my mailbox, they contained what was, for me, new scenes!

In the midst of all this, I'd started dating a girl named Jill. We'd been friends before that, yet she'd never seen my dorm room because we typically hung out at her suite. So once our friendship blossomed into something more, I began to worry. See, I *liked* this girl. And in my obsessive-compulsive need to collect all things Starfleet, I… may have gone a bit overboard.

My friends' rooms were decorated with heavy-metal bands, sports cars, Cindy Crawford, Kathy Ireland, beer logos, and adorable kittens doing adorably kitteny things. I, meanwhile, had turned my room into a giant-size *Trek* thing, and so, as we walked to my dorm, all I could think of was that Jill would take one look at Klingons and Vulcans plastered floor to ceiling, then turn and run away as though I'd instructed her to place the lotion in the basket. Instead, she just looked around, softly said "Woahhh..." and flashed me an amused "Well, you do you" grin. Then she continued into the room, boldly going where no Jill had gone before. Our wedding took place six years later.

Jill never became a fan (though she has watched it with me from time to time), and neither did my dad, stepmom, or sisters. Oddly enough, my brother Scott, who'd never embraced sci-fi throughout our lives, suddenly became a major fan in just the past few years, binging hundreds of episodes at a time. When he told me he'd become a die-hard Trekkie, my brain couldn't process it. It's been wild to geek out with him after a lifetime of being such different people. Meanwhile, my nephew Danny, raised by Jody in our mom's home, enjoyed *The Original Series* with his grandmother, creating a three-generational lineage that I'd failed to inspire with my own kids, Emily and Josh.

My mom passed away a few years ago, and it's been bittersweet to watch each new *Trek* show without her. She loved every iteration from *The Original Series* to *Discovery*, and throughout the years she and I watched all thirteen films in theaters, so it's sad to think she'll never see what's coming out now or in the future. Maybe my nephew will catch up on all the spinoffs, including those Mom never experienced. Maybe he, too, will turn his dorm room into a giant-size *Trek* thing and meet the space-girl of his space-dreams somewhere beyond the rim of starlight.

As for me, I'm content reliving memories of a mother-son fandom-sharing, of a bookstore tantrum that led to a guilty pleasure, of a kid brother loving a cartoon because his older sibling watched it, of another brother realizing in adulthood that *Star Trek* had been cool all along, of a girlfriend willing to explore strange new worlds with her strange new beau, and of a recurring fight with a sister over control of the TV each day after school. Ah, good times, good times. (No! *Star Trek*!)

Rich Handley (richhandley.com) has written, edited, or contributed to dozens of books, not only about *Star Trek* but also *Planet of the Apes, Watchmen, Back to the Future, Star Wars, Battlestar Galactica, Hellblazer, Swamp Thing, Stargate, Dark Shadows,* and other franchises. He edited Eaglemoss' *Star Trek Graphic Novel Collection*, helped IDW reprint the classic *Star Trek* comic strips, and contributed to IDW's *Star Trek 400th Issue*, and he has written for *Star Trek Communicator* and *Star Trek Explorer* magazines.

MRS. MALLON'S ENTERPRISE

BY JOHN S. DREW

P-H-I-L-C-O

The letters were etched in a silver script-like font on the surface of a white freezer door of the refrigerator that sat in the small kitchen of a Bronx apartment of our next-door neighbor, Mrs. Mallon. Being the oldest of four children, and four children who came one right after the other a year apart, I often found myself being ignored as my mother would care for my younger siblings. I often had to fend for myself when it came to getting any sort of adult affirmation that I was doing anything right.

And that came from Mrs. Mallon. The silver-haired elderly woman lived right across the hall from our third-floor apartment. There wasn't a day when I was five that I didn't find myself wandering over to the big, imposing red door with 3B stenciled on the front, and knocking to see if she was home.

She always welcomed me, no matter her physical state at the time. I think living alone as a widower, she enjoyed my company. And she was the person who ignited my love of reading. She didn't do it with simple "readers" of the time. I wasn't reading "See, Spot, run" or "Jim has the blue ball." I was reading the newspaper. Every day, Mrs. Mallon had her copy of the Daily News, usually brought to her by my father, sitting on the kitchen table. We read the comics. We read *Brenda Star* and *Dondi* and *Beetle Bailey*. I developed my early love of comics thanks to sitting there and reading and discussing the stories that unfolded within the tabloid's pages.

And when I say we, I mean me. I had to read it to her. She would help sound out the words I struggled with, but she insisted I do the reading. We'd sit at the kitchen table and read the paper. If there was a word she thought I should know more about, she would pull out the dictionary and we'd look up the definition. She also insisted I learn how to spell.

And once again, it wasn't "cat" or "dog" or "ball" that I was learning. I was spelling complex words, developing phonetic skills as I did. PHILCO, the name of the refrigerator brand, was one word Mrs. Mallon would often come back to in her testing of my spelling ability, covering up the word with her hand as I recited the letters.

There were two rewards when I succeeded at the tasks given me. One was lunch or dinner at Mrs. Mallon's, also a treat as she often would prepare meals I wanted instead of me having to eat what was offered at home, usually fare prepared at the request of my younger sisters.

I was spoiled by the lady, but we had a relationship akin to grandchild and grandmother. I knew there was a reward for completing the tasks, but there was also just the reward of spending time with this woman who focused on me. And I have to admit that made all the difference in the kind of person I am today.

There was one other reward.

In a house of four kids, a mother and a father and only one television set, your chances of watching what you wanted were about as slim as having a meal prepared that you liked. Dad worked a rotating shift of mornings one week, afternoons one week and overnights another week. It meant that when he was home, he was the king of the television. When he wasn't, my sisters were the queens of the television. Often, we watched *Sesame Street* or *Electric Company*, but then there were times they wanted to watch other programming that didn't appeal to me.

But with Mrs. Mallon, whenever I completed a learning task to her satisfaction, I had control of the television—to an extent. She made sure I never watched anything that could hurt my young psyche, but she was open to view something first to see if it was appropriate. We would finish the reading or the spelling task, have a bite of dinner and then she would take me into the living room and turn on her thirteen-inch color television.

We'd wait a moment as the old set warmed up, the image fading into view. I was a strange five-year-old kid. I liked watching the evening news, in particular, *Eyewitness News* at six. The program ran on channel seven here in New York with Roger Grimsby and Bill Beutel as the anchors. We would discuss the news as the two men reported it. Mrs. Mallon struck a nice balance when treating me as the child I was, while still speaking to me as an adult. She never talked down to me.

We'd follow watching the evening news by watching *The Price is Right* with host Dennis James. It was here another love of mine developed: game shows. Mrs. Mallon loved the show herself and she often would call out her guesses on the prizes being offered. By watching the show with her and seeing her play along, I developed a sense of value when it came to merchandise from groceries to high end items.

The news being the news, not all stories are appropriate for a young kid. When that happened, Mrs. Mallon would switch to another channel. To the young folks reading this, television sets didn't often come with a remote control. You had to get up from the couch and turn a knob to the channel you wished to watch. *Eyewitness News* was on channel seven, WABC. It was a quick change to move the dial to channel five, WNEW. There, *Bewitched* and *The Partridge Family* played during the news hour. Both were safe comedy fare for its time.

But there came a fateful day, when we switched to channel five and there was some special programming on that I can't remember what it was, for the life of me. Channels 2 and 4 had news as well, but I only liked the team of Grimsby and Beutel. So, Mrs. Mallon turned the dial in the opposite direction.

Channel nine, WWOR was showing *The Untouchables*. Mrs. Mallon quickly moved on as I caught a quick glimpse of mobsters getting mowed down by Elliot Ness and his team in black and white. She stopped at channel eleven, WPIX.

Mrs. Mallon had a color television. The news never seemed that vibrant on screen. There was something very colorful about *The*

Price is Right from the plaid jackets of host Dennis James to the evening gowns of the Showcase ladies to the set design itself. But there was something very different about what was being shown on channel eleven.

The first thing I noticed was the bright purple sky. I had never considered the sky could be purple and yet here it was as men in colored shirts—red, blue and gold—moved about the surface of an alien planet while being pursued by a woman who could kill them with her touch. The scene shifted as I saw the vessel that brought them there moving through space, trying to return to retrieve them.

I fell in love.

I literally fell in love with that ship. I had seen spaceships before, having watched the various Buster Crabbe *Flash Gordon* serials on our public television station, Channel 13, but this was different. It didn't look like a tank or a bullet or a rocket for that matter. It was distinctive as it cut through space with a mighty whoosh. (I didn't know at the time it really shouldn't have done that since there is no sound in the vacuum of space.)

And then the scene shifted to the interior of the ship, the bridge, and there I noticed the strange man with the pointed ears. He was in charge, ordering those on the bridge including a woman of color who handled communications throughout the ship.

For Mrs. Mallon, the pointed ears were too much. He was demonic. I would have nightmares about the man. Admittedly, she had a point. I used to have nightmares about "Thing" from *The Addams Family*. I would dream that there were multiple hands coming out of everywhere and would grab me and pull me apart. (Couldn't watch *The Addams Family* for years.)

I begged and pleaded for her not to change the channel. I promised I wouldn't let the pointy-eared man get to me. She looked doubtful, but she settled into the couch next to me, muttering how my father would kill her if I woke him up in the middle of the night with my screams when he needed to be in to work early in the morning.

The show, of course, was *Star Trek*. The episode was "That Which Survives." Admittedly, not the best episode to introduce a new viewer to, but as a five-year-old, the colors, the special effects, the interaction between the characters and that beautiful ship, the *Enterprise*, were more than enough to hook me in.

There was one other feature of this show that cinched my love for it—Lee Meriwether. She played the woman who would unfold herself, touch one of the crewmembers, killing them, before folding herself back and disappearing. Lee Meriwether…she was Catwoman! Before my love for *Star Trek*, there was *Batman*, and the Caped Crusaders episodes aired on WPIX for many years, often just before *Star Trek*. And there was a *Batman* movie that would air from time to time on the *4:30 Movie* on channel seven. And Lee Meriwether was Catwoman. If *Star Trek* was good enough for Catwoman, it got my support.

I went home that night jabbering away about the show to my parents, my siblings, the cat—anyone that would give me a moment to listen before turning away. Because that was the sad part of it all. Save for Mrs. Mallon, no one in my family was remotely interested in this incredibly cool show I had discovered.

I broached the subject with my friends at school and found a lukewarm reception. They were aware of the show, but they weren't as excited about it like I was—that is, save for one individual, Andrew. He knew the show. He had the Mego figures. He never said anything because he was afraid the other kids would laugh at him. (Remember, this was a time before it was hip to be into anything fantastic.)

He and I would talk about episodes of the show that I managed to catch at Mrs. Mallon's. He invited me to his house, and we played with his figures and his Mego Bridge Playset. Between us, we managed to convince a few of our friends to check out the show and they became fans. We would play *Star Trek* during recess.

And it was here that the next part of my *Star Trek* journey took place. As we played, my friends would call dibs on characters. Someone was Kirk. Someone was Spock.

"Who are you going to be, John?"

"I want to be the guy who puts the words in their mouth."

One of the things I also noticed as I became more engaged in the show was the names that would flash on the screen at the start and end of the show: Gene Roddenberry, Gene Coon, D. C. Fontana, David Gerrold. If I liked an episode, I made a point to remember who had a hand in producing it and I saw a pattern. I noted the greater humor and social commentary of stories by David Gerrold while I watched the greater character development in stories by D.C. Fontana.

And I knew this was something I wanted to do.

I would write up scenarios that my friends would then act out in the playground. They were simple things, but based on my friends' response, it encouraged me to write more. As I grew older, I would write stories based on *Star Trek*, *Batman*, and *The Six Million Dollar Man*. Sadly, none of these opuses exist anymore, but I have the fond memory of one story in which the *Enterprise* catapulted to the past and helped Steve Austin and Bigfoot when Nedlick, an enemy alien, tried to invade Earth.

I eventually moved from writing what was basically fan fiction and tried my hand at getting into the professional field. In the 80s, DC Comics produced a *Star Trek* comic featuring the cast of the show set in the movie timeline. I was sixteen years old. I found the mailing address for the company and knew that Robert Greenberger was the then editor of the series. I put together a story pitch for a single issue called "Saavik's First Command" and sent it along.

A few weeks later, I received a reply and was shocked to see it was not the form letter I often heard writers receive. Bob Greenberger wrote a personal letter, breaking down what worked and what didn't work in the pitch. And he didn't finish it by saying, "good luck with your future endeavors." He suggested I try again.

And I did. For the next two-three years, I would send Bob various story ideas and he always responded with a personal letter on DC stationary. Eventually, I had to move on because I was heading off to college and I found that my time to write was spent more on papers and creative writing projects. Years later, Bob informed me if I had just kept at it, I would have had a chance at a replacement slot because I was getting it. (Lesson, kids: never give up.)

During this time, the movies were playing in theaters, and it was always exciting to go to the theater and see *Star Trek* on the big screen. That was, until *Star Trek III: The Search for Spock*. As the movie came to its exciting conclusion, the Enterprise reached the planet Genesis and the title of the movie being fulfilled, James T. Kirk made, what I consider, the ultimate sacrifice, the destruction of the Enterprise in order to stop the Klingons from obtaining the secret of Genesis.

Call me crazy, when Spock died in *Star Trek II*, I didn't shed a tear. Watching the saucer section explode and the vessel fall to the surface of Genesis as a fireball in *Star Trek III* left me bawling like a baby. As I sat there in the theater, I was reminded of my time with Mrs. Mallon as we first discovered the show and her concerns over Mr. Spock to her bemoaning when an episode we'd already seen would be on and I would insist we had to watch it. It sounds crazy, but when the Enterprise was destroyed, my childhood died with it.

For so many people, *Star Trek* is a cultural phenomenon. It speaks to social and political issues that are relevant to so many people. It's a great action series and has characters that almost everyone can connect with in some way or another. But for me, it's a TV show, like so many others I grew up with and became attached to, that helped shape and define the person I am today.

I did get to see my *Trek* fiction professionally published. Years later, I had an opportunity, thanks to friend and editor Keith R.A. DeCandido, to have a story published for the *Star Trek S.C.E. (Starfleet Corps of Engineers)* line. "Paradise Interrupted" was a story of technical issues on the planet Risa causing chaos as the Gorn looked for a rogue sentient energy source. It wasn't Kirk, Spock and McCoy, but it was *Star Trek* as now-Captain Scott assigned tasks to the crew of the *USS da Vinci*.

There has been so much *Star Trek* since then from new series to comics to novels to games, it's hard to keep up with sometimes. But in the end, the core, the heart of the entire franchise, will always be The Original Series. Boldly going forward where no one has gone before. And I am a better person for watching it, all those years ago.

John S. Drew has been a doorman, restaurant manager, writer, teacher, podcaster and hostage negotiator at one point or another in his life. He has written prose in the *Star Trek*, Doctor Who and Spider-Man universes. He podcasts about pop culture, in particular television adventures of the '60s and '70s, including The Batcave Podcast, The Shazam/Isis Podcast, The OSI Files (about the Six Million Dollar Man and The Bionic Woman), The World's Greatest Super Friends Podcast (with Dan Greenfield), and The Doctor's Beard (about Doctor Who, with Jim Beard). You can find all these podcasts on any reputable or less than reputable podcast platform.

MY EARLY TREKS WITH CAPTAIN KURT

BY ALAN J. PORTER

"The Universe Star Ship Enterprise *left Earth's atmosphere to embark on a five-year deep space exploration. Massive in proportion and manned by thousands, the* Enterprise's *mission is to make peaceful contact with any form of life in the Universe.*

"After many adventures, Captain Kurt computes the ship's log: Captain's log, star date 24.09.45. Proceeding on star mapping mission. All has been quiet for five months.

"On the bridge are Navigator Bailey, Helmsman Sulu, and the strange Mr. Spock, the super intelligence of the Enterprise.

"Bailey: Interference on navigational laser beam.

"Spock: Hold it steady. Mr. Sulu.

"Sulu: Steady it is.

"Suddenly the vast space ship shudders."

So began my first encounter with *Star Trek*. It was January 18th, 1969, and I had just picked up the first issue of a new comic entitled *Joe 90 Top Secret*.

Joe 90 was the newest puppet supermarionation production from Century 21 productions, the home of Gerry Anderson's amazing run of puppet-based science fiction shows. I was nine years old and had grown up on Gerry Anderson's shows, from *Supercar*, to *Fireball XL5*, *Stingray*, and of course *Thunderbirds* and my personal favorite *Captain Scarlet*. The characters and their fantastic vehicles from all these shows appeared in a shared universe within the pages of *TV21* comic, a must read for me and my friends.

But his latest show, *Joe 90*, featuring a nine-year-old boy who was brainwashed by his adopted father and sent on secret missions, was set in a different time frame and didn't fit in the shared universe framework. So, Joe got his own comic. One that would also include strips related to various other shows that Century 21 had by a quirk of fate picked up the UK comics rights for.

Several years previously a US comics publisher had printed an unauthorized *Supercar* strip in one of its titles. After some negotiation it was agreed that in recompense that Century 21 Publications would have reciprocal UK markets rights to the US series the American publisher held, and that included any show produced by Desilu productions.

So it was that the first issue of *Joe 90 Top Secret* included a four-page adventure for its title star, along with the obligatory soccer themed strip and sports star pin-up pages, several "Super TV Strips" *The Champions* (a British live-action adventure series[1] not related to the Anderson universe) and two American shows that had yet to air in the UK, *Land of the Giants*, and in the prime center spread location something called *Star Trek*.

"*Spock: Check all instruments… I want a full report and get me Captain Kurt.*

"*Kurt is in his quarters: What's going on up there, Mr. Spock?*

"*Spock on speaker: Main computer reports a cosmic storm from a super nova. All instruments green and functional.*

"*Kurt: Keep me informed, Mr. Spock… I'll be in the gym.*

"*Captain's Log*" 24.10.57 - *72 minutes since the Enterprise was struck by the cosmic storm.*

"*Bailey: Course still pre-set and normal.*

"*Sulu: Star cameras normal.*

"*Captain Kurt is suddenly on the bridge: Something wrong, Mr. Spock?*

"*Spock: I'm not sure, Captain… Project the last ten star shots simultaneously.*

"*The pictures, taken over the last four hours, are superimposed on to each other.*

[1] Often overlooked as perhaps the first live-action no-capes super hero show as it featured three intelligence operatives gifted with strange powers

"Kurt: They're all the same. The camera's shooting the same picture over and over again.

"Spock: With your permission Captain, I'd like to put out a repair crew to check the aerial."

I had no idea who these people were, but I was captivated from the moment I turned the page and was presented with a colorful two page spread by artist Harry Linfield (not that I knew that then as British comics back then didn't carry credits), with its use of vibrant colors and diverse panel shapes and layouts. At the time the UK had a tradition of great science-fiction and space-based strips that were rightly renowned for dynamic, vibrant art and innovative page layouts and panel design[2].

And of course, there was another fantastic vehicle to appreciate. The sleek saucer shape atop a cylindrical fuselage and the two rockets sitting aft on those raked pylons. This was one cool looking spaceship.

Captain Kurt seemed to be a cool guy too, although a bit laid back in his command style, preferring to head to the gym than find out what was happening. But who was this Spock person, and what made him "the super intelligence of the *Enterprise*"? Did he have super powers? Was he somehow connected to the ship itself? I had to keep reading.

"Repair crew bay. Kurt on speaker: This is the Captain. Exterior repair crews will report to exit tubes to carry out repairs to the star camera aerial.

"Guy in spacesuit[3]: That's us. Prepare the Repair Wagon.

"Exterior shot of the Enterprise: VO: Repair Wagon's launched… and thanks for putting the Enterprise in orbit Captain.

"Bridge: Spock: Orbit around what, Jackson?

"Jackson on video screen: Some joke, Captain. But just to keep the record straight, I'd say it was a planet twice the size of Earth.

"Kurt: What's wrong with Jackson? Is he sick?

"Spock: Maybe Captain … But I'll take a look with my own eyes. Open Observation port!

"A panel slides aside to reveal a mammoth window.

---

[2] I was unaware at the time of the existence of the early American *Star Trek* comics published by Gold Key. Studying them two years later the Gold Key pages look flat and dull in comparison.
[3] The space suits and several ancillary craft designs are clearly 'borrowed' from the 2001 movie

"Spock: It's incredible.

"Kurt: Why didn't we have any advance warning?

"Spock looking at ticker tape output: The computer is not registering the planet! All systems reject the planet's existence!"

And so ended the first week's installment. Yes, the dialog was hokey, the timelines in the captions and dialog don't add up, and the idea that no-one could notice a planet until they looked out a window seemed daft[4] even to nine-year old me.

It turned out that the mystery planet was populated entirely by robots who then invited the *Enterprise* to land (yes, land) and have the crew disembark down gangways while the Captain and Spock used the Captain's shuttle that detached from the bottom of the saucer section[5]. The robots end up holding the crew hostage in return for the use of some of the power rods from the *Enterprise*'s engines. Kirk (midway through the story the Captain's name is corrected without explanation) sabotages the rods and uses them to wipe out the robot inhabitants in a nuclear explosion. What's a little genocide between friends—they were only sentient robots after all. Prime Directive? Never heard of it.

As you can probably guess from the extracts above the writer, or writers, of these early strips, unfortunately their names were never documented[6], had clearly never seen an episode of *Star Trek*.

Popular culture in the UK in the late 1960s reflected the dichotomy of a society struggling to cross generational boundaries. Even as a nine-year-old I was aware of the tensions between the UK of the swinging-sixties psychedelic generation and those who just a decade before had lived through the austerity of a country recovering from a devastating conflict. As I was growing up, memories of rationing were still fresh[7], and the landscape was still littered with the occasional bomb-site of rubble left as the result of an air raid twenty years previously.

While the 1950s in the US were seen as a time of prosperity where the dreams of taking manifest destiny to the stars held sway, in the UK it was a time of rebuilding and reconstruction. Space and

---

[4]I loved the fact that they used a similar idea in a recent episode of *Picard*!
[5]Another idea from this strip that was ahead of its time - see *Star Trek: Insurrection*
[6]The strips that appeared in Joe 90: Top Secret are sometimes attributed to writer Angus Allen.
[7]Rationing was eventually discontinued in 1954, a full nine-years after the end of World War II.

aerospace technology wasn't about exploring, it was about defense. So it was that the British version of *Star Trek* in the comics was less "wagon train to the stars," and more a "Royal Air Force in space."

On July 26th, 1969, the *Enterprise* took over the front cover of issue #28 of *Joe 90 Top Secret* with a dynamic shot of it in flight around a planet, (with what looked like exhaust gasses coming from the nacelles!) accompanied by the headline, "TV's Great New Series - *Star Trek* - Inside!"

In fact, the show had already debuted on the BBC on July 12th, and for some of us it had been a long six months of waiting.

What a revelation it was, sure the comic strips so far had been fun, and for those young things that had been reading them, we sort of knew who these characters were, but the show itself was eye opening. The sets and special effects were clearly in a different orbit than the ones we were used to with British live action science fiction shows such as *Doctor Who* which was still in black and white at that point.

Color TV had only been introduced in the UK two years prior and was only just beginning to become mainstream in British homes. I recall that in July 1969 we still had a black and white set and that I made a special trip across the road to my friend John's house to watch *Star Trek* on his parent's fancy color set. It became a weekly pilgrimage for me, and for about twelve months, until we got our own set, *Star Trek* was the only show I watched in color.

Even after the show debuted on the BBC the *Star Trek* of the comics continued on their own path, so that for the next few years I got to experience two parallel *Star Trek*s. Perhaps my earliest introduction to the concept of multiverse, (even though no one used that term back then).

Perhaps the most striking aspect of the British *Star Trek* stories is the shift in the crew dynamics. Dr. McCoy is rarely used. Spock takes on the role of the central identification character, perhaps an underlying empathic resonance with the traditional British reserve and "stiff upper lip" national identity. Scotty, as the only British crew member, is often portrayed as the action hero.

This Captain Kurt/Kirk, far removed from the brash confident commander portrayed by William Shatner, is an effective and somewhat rash leader. More than half the stories are instigated as a result of Kirk being an idiot.

In contrast to the ineffectual James T. Kirk, the Spock of these stories is sometimes close to being Superman. His powers and abilities are many and varied, serving whatever the story needs without regard to established character, or, somewhat ironically, internal story logic, jumping between being a scientist, computer expert, engineer, and doctor with ease.

The Montgomery Scott of this *Enterprise* is as much a warrior as he is an engineer. In many ways he takes over Kirk's role in that he is clearly a better combat officer and leader. He also replaces Dr. McCoy as the supporting arm of the lead triumvirate.

Even our aliens were different, for instance the Romulans weren't pointy eared distant cousins of the Vulcans, instead we had a race of Roman Centurions that operated in something called The Pirate Zone[8].

All these variants made reading the strips a fun experience. It was a different universe, with different rules (at times it seemed it actually didn't have any rules) than the TV show. At times hints of the swinging Sixties would creep through (a race of giant talking mushrooms[9]), but the undertone was still very much one of the wistful echoes of an empire lost and the rose-tinted view of the perceived glories of the recent conflict.

It was the TV show that gave us a sense of hope and wonder. It was there we really started to explore the final frontier. The comics stories were fun, but it was the TV stories that captured my imagination in a way that nothing else had before. Even at nine going on ten I knew that beneath the surface they were addressing deeper issues than just having fun space adventures.

And there was the action. It didn't take long before John and I would spend hours playing *Star Trek*. He lived on a corner lot so had a bigger yard, and it was there that we explored our own strange new worlds. There was always something that made us stagger around his lawn the way the bridge crew did when the *Enterprise* was suddenly

[8]TV 21 #82-90 (17th April to 12th June 1971) - writer and artist unknown
[9]Valiant & TV21 #19-22 (29th January to 26th February 1972) - writer unknown / artist John Stokes

gripped by some unknown force. The same lawn would also be the location for numerous Kirk combat rolls.

Those were great innocent times, and I thank the original series for those memories, and the worlds of imagination and science it opened up for me. I've always maintained that it was Gerry Anderson that made me into an engineer, and *Star Trek* that made me a writer.

I had decided at the age of eight that, despite my problems with spelling, I wanted to be a writer someday. Stories had become important to me, and I watched my favorite shows with increasing interest as I started to try and figure out why certain TV shows, comics, and books held my attention. *Star Trek* was soon among those that I thought about even after the end credits rolled.

But my memories of early Trek will always be dominated by the comics. Even when the show started to air, they continued to tell stories with a distinctly British flavor. You were just as likely to find stories where the *Enterprise* crew taught sentient apes to play soccer[10], or Kirk and Spock end up in World War Two fighter planes[11], as you were space battles.

The strips lasted longer than the show's initial run on the BBC[12], running across different title mergers from 1969 to 1973. From *Joe 90 Top Secret* to the combined *TV21 & Joe 90*, the TV21 itself, until that merged with *Valiant*. In all there were 37 original *Star Trek* adventures told with a unique British flavor[13].

Over the years I have experienced hundreds of episodes across every TV incarnation of *Star Trek*, watched all the movies, read numerous Trek related novels and studied all the comics series from different publishers. Through all of that, certain scenes and images from the early British comics strips have always stayed with me. In many ways, they are my personal Original *Star Trek*. This is where my own ongoing exploration of the final frontier began.

---

[10]Joe 90: Top Secret #11-14 (29th March to 16th April 1969) - writer Angus Allen? / artist Harry F. Linfield
[11]Valiant & TV21 #23-33 (4th March to 13th May 1972) - writer unknown / artist John Stokes
[12]12th July 1969 to 15th December 1971
[13]For more details on the British *Star Trek* Comics check out my book *Star Trek: A Comics History* - Hermes Press, 2009, or my essay "Flaming Nacelles & Giant Snails" in *New Life and New Civilizations: Exploring Star Trek Comics* - Sequart (2014). - You can read the stories themselves in the three-volume series *Star Trek: The Classic UK Comics* from IDW / Library of American Comics.

Alan J. Porter writes about stuff and makes up stories too. From the worlds of pop-culture to high adventure fiction, and the occasional comics project. You can keep up with his various scribblings either via his website at alanjporter.com or on Twitter @alanjporter.

A GAME FOR THE YOUNG

BY BOBBY NASH

The 1970s. The distant frontier.

It wasn't the Starship *Enterprise* that carried young Commander Bobby Nash (who wanted to be an ensign?) to and from his various adventures. No, sir. It was a big, yellow and black school bus belonging to the Gwinnett County School System. Not as elegant a conveyance as a Starfleet vessel, but it got the job home. Every afternoon, I was excited to see that big ugly bus because I knew it was taking me home where my mother waited with a hug and an after-school snack prepared. It also meant I would soon be beaming aboard the USS *Enterprise* for an adventure before my mom sent me on a landing party outside to play.

And play I did. For me, the final frontier was the family backyard. I grew up in Doraville, Georgia. Calling Liberty Heights, the community we called home, the poor section of town was being generous at best, but it was an okay place to grow up. The tiny community had been built near Georgia's General Motors Assembly Plant, which is no longer there. Hey, Doraville even had a song sung about it ("…touch of country in the city," indeed) so it couldn't have been too bad, right?

In my memory, Casa de Nash sported a huge backyard that seemed to go on forever and ever. Seeing that same piece of property years later as an adult, I realized that it was your standard half-acre tract, a tiny front yard with a narrow backyard that stretched a good ways back from the house. It had all the building blocks that my imagination turned into whatever backdrop I needed that day. A large sandy area was perfect for playing with my Matchbox cars, cut off tree stumps became planets that I landed the spaceships I made out of spare pieces of wood and plastic I found around the yard. The fallen tree and small concrete retaining wall became rooftops and walls to jump over with my bionic powers. The treehouse at the far back was the bridge of my spaceship that took me to all those places I could only dream of going. The building where the lawnmower lived was an alien castle. My dad's old '63 ½ Ford Fastback was a racecar or a getaway vehicle when I felt the need for speed. The swing set and jungle gym were stand-ins for whatever my imagination needed. It was especially good for crossing pools of hot lava. Plus, there was that one small section of the backyard none of us ever ventured into. I still don't understand why. It was always avoided. Maybe monsters lived there. Who knows?

Growing up as an only child (my brother, Wes didn't show up until I was eight and a half), my childhood playmate was my imagination. That imagination was a troublemaker, let me tell ya. Like Calvin and his pet tiger, Hobbes, I caught a lot of grief for it from my parents, friends, and relatives. They all seemed to think I was weird at best, troubled at worst. Maybe they were on to something as there have been some kooky ideas spewed forth from my brain over the years, let me tell ya. I'll leave it to history to decide the merits of my sanity. Ha! Ha! But I digress… It was not uncommon for young Bobby to run around the family backyard pretending to swing through the city with *Spider-Man* (my mom loved telling stories of me running around making the web-shooter noise and hearing her repeat the sound always cracked me up), fighting crime with Batman, going on secret missions with the Six Million Dollar Man or Buck Rogers, stopping speeders like Ponch and Jon when I rode my bike, but most of the time, I found myself beaming down to an alien planet that resembled my back yard with Captain Kirk and company.

Now, I wasn't content to just reenact the episode I watched. Oh, no. I started crafting new stories, new planets, new aliens, and various troubles that I could get into along with the crew of the USS *Enterprise*. I've often mentioned that these early days at play had a major impact on my becoming a writer, even though I didn't know it at the time. *Star Trek* definitely falls into that category, but we'll come back to that a little bit later.

What initially attracted me to *Star Trek* was the action, the adventure, the monsters, the aliens, and the bright colors, but I immediately felt a bond with the characters that made up the crew of the Starship *Enterprise*. They became friends, people I cared about, that I rooted for, even. Without realizing it, I learned lessons of tolerance, forgiveness, cooperation, teamwork, and more from these fictional characters. As a kid, many of those concepts flew right by me as I *fangoobered* (another word I wasn't aware of way back when) over the cool effects and creatures, but the beauty of this series, nay, this franchise, is that I can watch episodes again decades later and discover nuances I missed on previous viewings.

Part of this is because of my own experiences. The Bobby that watched *Star Trek* as a kid, the Bobby who watched as a teenager, in his twenties, thirties, or even now in his—*gasp!*—fifties, all get something different from the experience. That, I've learned in my writing career, is one of the basics of good storytelling. *Star Trek* has layers. Lots and lots of layers.

Before I discovered *Star Trek*, I had already expressed an interest in exploration. I read books on all things outer space, myths and legends, ancient histories, and the like. Daydreams of discovering some hidden land or unknown thing occupied my creative thoughts. How cool would it be to be an explorer, I wondered. Sadly, my parents refused to book travel passage for their six-year-old son to the Amazon rainforest. Buzzkills.

Then, I saw *Star Trek* for the first time and the fact that they were explorers boldly going to strange new worlds, as they did, truly resonated with me. These characters on this TV show were doing the things I had only dreamt of up to this point. Since my parents were not about to let me leave the confines of our backyard, watching the adventures of the *Enterprise* crew allowed me to explore vicariously through them. All I needed was my imagination and our backyard.

From there, my interest in real world studies of exploration grew. I became fascinated not only with outer space, but with NASA and how rockets were built and worked. I was fascinated with the *Space Lab* station in orbit and was sad when it crashed back to Earth. I watched TV shows on the unknown and unexplained. The fact that Mr. Spock himself hosted a series called *In Search Of...* only stoked the flames of this desire to learn more about the unknown. I had questions. Lots and lots of questions. How could we live in space? Could this future that *Star Trek* showed us really happen? I wanted to know, and more importantly, I wanted to be part of it. I needed to be part of it.

Sadly, the real world interfered and altered the course of my life, as it is wont to do. I grew up, found competing interests; comic books, Star Wars, girls (who didn't think the first few things on this list were cool), then came jobs, cars, bills, you know, those things. Heh. Through it all, *Star Trek* remained important to me. When I started focusing my attention on writing and drawing, creating my own stories, there was always a dream of writing my own *Star Trek* stories. In fact, in elementary school, a friend and I did just that. We wrote and drew a *Star Trek* comic together. I would do a page, hand it off and he would do the next, then back to me. I have only the tiniest memories of this, but I can imagine the story was all over the place because we were just having fun and doing whatever we wanted. It was fun and intrigued me to continue creating my own comics with my own characters, many derivative versions of what I already knew, but expanding and, hopefully, improving. We'll swing back around to that in a minute.

If you're reading this, I assume you know the show, the characters, and the episodes so I'm not going to rehash that which you know so well. Doesn't mean I won't stick in a little inside joke though. Here's what these characters meant to me.

From Captain James T. Kirk, I learned leadership skills. One of the things I respected about the captain was his ability to be a tough, stern leader, but he also had a friendly rapport with his crew. They struck me as friends. Seeing how the character straddled the line between commanding officer and just one of the guys informed a good deal of my opinions on leadership. Many of those qualities I took with me when I found myself in leadership positions later in life. I would wonder how my childhood hero might handle a situation. Once I removed the punching and ripping shirt part from the equation, Jim Kirk's example usually offered sound advice.

Mr. Spock and Mr. Scott were the brains. There was a time in my life where I considered studying the sciences. This path derailed rather quickly, especially once I learned how much math was involved in the sciences. Math and I were hardly ever on good terms. Despite my shortcomings in that regard, Spock and Scotty were clearly thinkers, men who were able to think up solutions based on formula, method, ingenuity, and perhaps a little bit of pulling it out of thin air, but the actors played it so convincingly that their characters believed it so therefore I believed it. I can absolutely understand how many fans were inspired by these characters to move into scientific fields. It staggers my brain to think about the number of advances in science, technology, and medicine that can be traced back to *Star Trek*. If nothing else, that alone gives the series a proud legacy.

My favorite character from the original series is Dr. Leonard "Bones" McCoy. It's hard not to like Bones. Not only is he good at his job, but he's probably the most human of the bunch. He was my way in. When Spock explains things to McCoy, he's also explaining them to me. Plus, and this is very important when it comes to these characters, is that even though Bones rarely got the last word, he did in fact get most of the best lines. This trend continued well into the movies as well. As something of a smart-alec myself, or so I was often informed, Bones was the coolest guy and quickly became my favorite. In fact, he's my second favorite character across the entire franchise, the top spot held by Chief Miles Edward O'Brien, but that's a story for another book.

Uhura, Sulu, Chekov, and the rest of the supporting cast were also impressive. One of the moments that stands out to me was during an emergency, Uhura leapt to the con station and took over navigation. I forget the episode as I am terrible at recalling names. Sorry. That was my first experience with cross-training. The crew were all good at their jobs but could also step in and do other jobs when needed. Seeing Scotty in command was another great example of this. Again, it was one of those things that, on my original viewing, didn't mean much, but later I would come to understand how important Uhura, Sulu, and Chekov being on that bridge was outside of the fictional *Star Trek* universe.

The 1970's were a bit turbulent in my memory. As a kid, there was a lot I didn't realize, especially as it related to the larger world issues such as politics, finances, and the like. I knew we didn't have much money, but I also knew we never went hungry. The things that stick out in my memory were closer to home. A gas shortage paralyzed the city and I remember the news showing cars lined up at stations that were out of gas. Atlanta dealt with a series of child murders, something that definitely scared me as a kid. The GM plant had layoffs which impacted my family as that's where my dad, grandfather, and uncles worked. The nearby gas refinery exploded, which did not help the gas shortage at all. The Klan marched through our neighborhood, burning crosses in yards and destroying property, a truly terrifying moment that remains etched in my brain to this day. There was also a murder in the neighborhood, followed by a heavy police presence that had not been present when the fires I mentioned earlier were raging. Oh, and then there was the adventure with the wild monkey loose in the neighborhood that lived in my backyard for a couple of weeks. That last one was, by far, the most pleasant of experiences until the end. But that's a story for another day.

I was still quite young when these events occurred. In truth, at that age, I was still fairly innocent in the ways of the world. I didn't have context for a lot of the things I witnessed, but I knew how to deal with fear thanks to *Star Trek*. I knew that heroes stood up for their friends and those who couldn't protect themselves. I wondered how these real people had not heard of the ideals of Infinite Diversity in Infinite Combinations. Where was man's love for man? These were questions that ran through my young brain. Sadly, there were not many answers forthcoming. In fact, now, all these decades later, I look around and see a world that could benefit from a little IDIC logic.

But this essay is meant to be uplifting so let me get back on track.

Star Trek's influence on me continued in reruns, books, comics, and my imagination, but it was a treasure that I enjoyed alone. My parents were not sci-fi fans in general, or *Star Trek* fans in particular. In fact, my mother had a rather intense dislike of Captain Kirk's alter ego, William Shatner. She never could explain it, but she would cut off a movie if she saw his name in the credits. Weird, I know. *Star Trek* was something that I loved alone, as far as I knew…until I turned twelve.

I was twelve when we moved. It was a tumultuous time for me. Moving was not something I wanted to do. This new unknown terrified me, but like the explorers I idolized, I looked on this move from the city to the country as though discovering a brave new world. I would finally become an explorer at last. This new perception of my reality made the move, and starting a new school weeks after it was already in process for everyone else easier. I was lucky. The first group of guys I met at my new school were into cool things like comic books, gaming, movies, Star Wars, and *Star Trek*.

At long last, I had found my people.

I often wonder if I would have eventually drifted away from my love of comics, sci-fi and *Star Trek* had we not moved at such a pivotal age. I suspect that my parents would have approved of that. They were never overly fond of my fandoms and actively tried to cut me off from them on multiple occasions. Odd then, that years later, they would come to appreciate my writing career, including some *Star Trek*-ish projects. Gotta love when these things happen, right?

I've never written *Star Trek* in any official capacity. Don't get me wrong, I would love to do something official with the property (just in case anyone with the power to make that happen is reading these words). It might happen. Never say never, right? The closest I've gotten to writing *Star Trek* is in an unofficial capacity.

I met the wonderful cast and crew of *Starship Farragut* at a convention. We sat across the aisle from one another, and I heard their episodes on loop all weekend. By the end of the con, I pitched them a story idea. They liked it and I started work on my first screenplay, a *Star Trek* fan film called "Conspiracy of Innocence" for *Starship Farragut*. The episode was filmed and distributed (it's on YouTube). A public screening was held at the studio where the sets resided, and

I went with a friend. You can't imagine the thrill of seeing the USS *Farragut* fly past the camera with "Written by Bobby Nash" on the screen. It is a great, fond memory. My love letter to the TV series that meant so much to me. It was a magical moment.

Since then, I've written a few more fan film scripts for various productions, including *Starship Farragut* ("Conspiracy of Innocence"), *Hospital Ship Marie Curie* ("Under Fire"), *Starship Webster* ("Where Monsters Dwell"), *Starship Deimos* ("Periphery"), and *Star Trek: Continues* ("Pilgrim of Eternity"), the latter of which included me writing dialogue for Kirk, Spock, McCoy, and the rest of the gang.

Finally, after all those years of dreaming about the final frontier, I found myself standing inside the USS *Enterprise*, walking her corridors, and even getting a chance to sit in the captain's chair. Let me tell you, it's a mighty comfy chair indeed.

Star Trek remains as important to me today as it was when I was a kid. Maybe even more as the little TV show that could spawn a couple of animated series, a movie franchise, and multiple spinoffs, offering me so many hours of entertainment that even made me think on occasion. At its best, *Star Trek* straddled the line between action/adventure and morality tale with skill and grace. Trust me, as someone who has attempted to write such things, that is no easy task, and I marvel at the amazing stories this universe has produced.

As we go into the future, I look forward to continuing to boldly go to all the brave new worlds, to all the undiscovered countries yet to be explored along with *Star Trek*.

I hope I'm up to the task.

Nash to *Enterprise*. One to beam up.

Energize.

Bobby Nash is not a man of action, a starship captain, or an alien, but he loves writing about those who are. Bobby is an award-winning author of novels, comic books, short stories, screenplays, audio, and more. He is a member of the International Association of Media Tie-in Writers, International Thriller Writers, and Southeastern

Writers Association. On occasion, he acts, appearing in movies and TV shows, usually standing behind or beside your favorite actor, but sometimes they even let him speak. For more information on Bobby Nash and his work, please visit him at www.bobbynash.com, www.ben-books.com, and across social media.

I WASN'T A TEENAGE STAR TREK FAN

BY TOM BREVOORT

You ask me about my memories of *Star Trek* from when I was growing up, and my first instinct is to say that I don't have any. For all that it seemed like it should have been an easy lay-up into my sensibilities, I never quite caught the *Star Trek* bug as a kid. Oh, sure, the series was ubiquitous, playing on New York's WPIX Channel 11 in the late afternoon/early evenings and on the weekends, and I was aware of it. But whenever I would tune in, I'd just find the show too ponderous for my tastes. Too much talking, too much standing around. I was a comic book kid, obsessed with super heroes. That's what I wanted in my entertainment. The characters in *Star Trek* struck me too much as being just people.

It probably didn't help things that I was never all that attracted to the show's main three actors. To be honest, I often found them exhausting, Shatner's broad performative interpretations as Captain Kirk, Nimoy's cold aloofness as Spock, and Kelly's straight up racism towards Mr. Spock as Doctor McCoy. (It was never framed in that way in the show, but let's face it, that's what it was.) I was much more attracted to the second team players: Sulu and Chekov and Uhura and Scotty. If the show had been about them more regularly, I probably would have tuned in more.

Now, the person in my family who was much more enamored of *Star Trek* was my younger brother Ken. He liked a bunch of things that held only limited appeal for me, such as monster movies and *Planet of the Apes*, and *Star Trek* was one of those things. This despite the fact that he was three years my junior and therefore even less worldly than I was. And in those days of antenna broadcast programming only, where our household only reliably received something in the neighborhood of six or seven stations, something was going to be playing at almost all times—because giving up control of the television meant that you didn't know when you might once again be able to get it back. So, I saw my fair share of *Star Trek* episodes growing up. Not all of them, and not completely, not even paying a whole lot of attention to them. But I absorbed the basic information about the franchise through osmosis.

The other person in my family who had a liking for *Star Trek* was my mother. She had watched it when it first ran on NBC, the same way she regularly tuned in for almost any science fiction or fantasy program that might come along: *Logan's Run*, *The Six Million Dollar Man*, *The Bionic Woman* (with its terrifying Fembots), *Lucan, the Man From Atlantis, Wonder Woman*, and everything else the era had to offer. She kept up a façade of normalcy but on the inside, she was a weirdo who liked these fanciful programs. And while *Star Trek* didn't loom large enough in her life to where she'd watch the reruns, she spoke well of it whenever the conversation came up. Like so many, she had a strong affinity for the mysterious Mister Spock, an affinity that remains to this day.

One of my strongest *Star Trek* memories of the era relates not to the television series, but to the first film, and is burned into my memory as though it happened only yesterday. The premiere of that film was a big deal in our household, and my Mom took her four kids to see it shortly after it opened in the twin-screen cinema located in the Waldbaum's shopping center where I'd occasionally buy three-in-a-bag comic books, as well as the Genovese drug store that sold out of date comics five-for-a dollar. Only a short way into the screening, as the characters began discussing the approaching threat of V'Ger, my mother had a brainstorm—she figured out the end twist. And so excited was she by this that she cried out at the top of her lungs, "V-Ger—Voyager! The Voyager Probe!" And every head in the theater turned in our direction, angrily. I honestly didn't think that we were going to make it out of that showing alive.

But as I say, *Star Trek* was everywhere in this era, and so it was impossible to ignore it. And certain episodes did capture my attention. In particular, I had a huge fascination with "The Menagerie." For one thing, it was a two-part episode, the only one in the run of the show. For another, it featured an almost completely different cast of characters than usual, as an extended flashback to earlier times before James T. Kirk came to command the Starship Enterprise. I had no understanding of pilot episodes or recouping sunken costs in those days, so I took everything at a surface level, and it was fascinating to me. Fascinating, but also disturbing. I can remember Captain Pike's horrifically burned and wheelchair-bound body making me wince a time or two, but it was the transformation of the beauteous Vina into her true scarred and misshapen form that truly horrified me. I didn't pay much heed to *Star Trek* episodes, but whenever "The Menagerie" came on in the background, I paid a lot more attention than usual.

I similarly had a strange soft spot for "Assignment: Earth," the *Star Trek* episode that really wasn't. Again, I had no understanding of the concept of a backdoor pilot. But I knew that I found this Gary Seven guy to be a lot more interesting than the usual players, especially when paired with Teri Garr's Roberta Lincoln. That whole episode strikes me now as something akin to a proto-*Doctor Who*, and so it's no wonder that I was drawn to it. Jon Pertwee would have made a wonderful Gary Seven, and Katy Manning is so Roberta Lincoln that it hurts.

Beyond that, there were other episodes, other moments, that stuck with me for some reason. I clearly remember the climax of "Devil in the Dark," where it turns out that the Horta creature that's been killing off miners is only doing so to protect its eggs and is as worthy of life and consideration as the human beings it's been in conflict with. I can recall the shenanigans of "Shore Leave," where Kirk is tormented by the dancing, laughing Finnegan, a rival from his Academy days. And of course, the finale of "City on the Edge of Forever," where to do the right thing, Kirk must do the wrong thing and prevent Dr. McCoy from saving the life of Edith Keeler. When I say that I wasn't a fan or a viewer, I mean that, and yet these bits, these moments, stuck with me regardless.

And while it would take me a while to connect all of the dots, I could eventually perceive the similarities between the Fantastic Four story that I first read in *Marvel's Greatest Comics* #72-75 (and which had first appeared in print years earlier in *Fantastic Four* #90-93) in which the mighty Thing is enslaved by the alien Skrulls and taken to a far-off planet where the culture has been based on the American "Roaring Twenties," and where he is expected to fight an arena duel against a similarly-powerful alien to secure territory claims for his new masters, and a pair of *Star Trek* episodes, "A Piece of the Action" and "Arena." Ben Grimm and his opponent Torgo even fought with oddly-shaped cudgels in emulation of Kirk and Spock in "Amok Time." Artist and plotter Jack Kirby was a regular viewer of *Star Trek* during its first run, and at the time he'd produced those stories, he was deliberately struggling to not give new characters and concepts to his employers at Marvel Comics. A short time earlier, he'd based a Doctor Doom storyline on the events of *The Prisoner*.

There were *Star Trek* comic books in this era as well, of course, strange things that were published by Gold Key, a company whose output was largely made up of licensed television properties. I mostly encountered these in early collected editions sold in department store toy sections. These books were sized and shaped like coloring books, and each one collected four issues of the comic book series. But even I could tell that they were seriously off-model; the Enterprise would sometimes be depicted on the painted covers with rocket flames venting from the backs of the ship's nacelles. I'd look through them simply because they were there, but nobody in my household ever took the plunge and bought one.

The same couldn't be said of the various *Star Trek* toys that came on the market during those days. That Genovese Drug Store I mentioned earlier also carried a large stock of affordably priced Mego action figures, posable dolls in the likenesses of the popular cinematic and comic book heroes of the day. I of course gravitated to the super heroes, never wavering in my devotion. But Ken went a different way, stocking up his toy chest with an assortment of *Star Trek* figures, among other things. He had a Captain Kirk and a Spock and a Klingon. They were really well-done figures for the era. Their likenesses were strong, and they each came with assorted weapons and props from the show, a tricorder and a phaser and communicator, the latter two fitting nicely into a plastic belt that would gird the figure's waist. And they'd cavort and caper and get involved in adventures alongside the astronauts and simians of *Planet of the Apes* and Batman and Green Arrow and Kid Flash and whoever else we happened to have on hand.

But the big item in the Mego *Star Trek* line was the full-scale Enterprise bridge playset, and he got one of those as well one Christmas. In retrospect, it isn't so impressive, constructed primarily of cardboard sealed in plastic (sort of in the way my Grandmother insisted on keeping her furniture.) and it all folded up into its own carrying case. But it had the Captain's command chair, and stations for the helm and navigation, and a series of vignettes that could be slotted into place on the ship's main viewscreen. But the big attraction was its transporter. It was a simple revolving door contraption with a pair of buttons at the top. You'd simply place your away team into the transporter, give it a spin with the top-mounted knob, and then press the down button. This would cause the spinning chamber to stop with the figures facing away from you, where they could be removed through a concealed doorway in the back of the set. By placing them back in, you could beam them back up again by giving another spin and pressing the up button. It was so simple that it was stupid, but it was also somehow the best action figure peripheral Mego ever produced. I loved that stupid thing, and it was endlessly entertaining to spin your guy and make him disappear and then reappear at the touch of a button.

I tended to mix-and-match our action figures into my own homebrewed super heroes, which is how both Spock and the Klingon wound up in one of my early attempts at making a full-length comic book. The group was called The Sentinels (though I mistakenly spelled it as The Sentinals) and it was comprised of Stretch Armstrong, a Planet of the Apes astronaut wearing Spock's uniform as The Web, Spock himself in the Klingon outfit, whom I'd given super-powers when he breathed in strange volcanic gasses in the manner of the Doom Patrol's Rita Farr, Kid Flash as pretty much himself, but called Kid Lightning and the Klingon shirtless as the gravity-manipulating Grav. I wrote and drew three full twenty-page issues, covers and interiors, starring these mismatched heroes, the first time I'd ever managed to complete a comic book story of my own that was full-length. They're unspeakably crude, of course, as I was only in grade school, but those books represented a step forward in my creative development.

I also got a set of the *Star Trek* communicator walkie-talkies when they were released. I had coveted walkie-talkies since seeing them used so often on television, and while the range on these little battery-powered units wasn't nearly what I would have liked it to be, they made up for that fact by being a pretty good emulation of the source material. It was cool to press the button and flip open the top of the thing James Kirk-style. Today, of course, they're way larger than even the least sophisticated smartphone—a piece of technology whose acceptance *Star Trek* paved the way for.

It wasn't really until the debut of *Star Wars* that *Star Trek* was eclipsed in the minds and hearts of my generation of kids. Tough to remember now, but the influence that the series had on mainstream science fiction-based media was relatively profound. In the world of comic books, past a certain point, every spaceship wound up being a derivation of the Enterprise, whether it was the Legion of Super Heroes' 30th Century Cruiser or the Guardians of the Galaxy's similar futuristic starship, the Captain America II. (It's perhaps no surprise that those two examples remain similar, as they were both designed by the great Dave Cockrum, one of the best super hero character designers of the era, who would gain great acclaim when he reinvented the X-Men alongside writer Len Wein but who would leave the book to draw the adaptation of the first *Star Trek* film.) The arrival of George Lucas' space-fantasy film changed all of that, but for about a decade, *Star Trek* was a primary influence in that four-color world.

Eventually, by the time I was in college, I wound up dating a girl for whom *Star Trek* was a seminal work, and so I wound up watching and appreciating the original series more. But it wasn't until *Star Trek: The Next Generation* that I truly became a *Star Trek* fan. I can remember her and I on a road trip somewhere discussing the names of the new characters that had been released and trying to make heads or tails of them. Geordi LaForge? Data? Tasha Yar? Deanna Troy? They seemed weird and alien to us, because *Star Trek* was so cemented in our minds as being Kirk, Spock and McCoy. Plus, those new names were just weird.

And I did purchase the VHS videotape of the restored *Star Trek* pilot, "The Cage," when it was initially offered in 1986, having been pieced back together from a black and white work print still in Gene Roddenberry's possession. I remember it being at once a haphazard affair and at the same time something I was desperately happy to see in its original form. That early pan-in on the Enterprise in flight that opens up into the first shot of the bridge is an image emblazoned on my memory.

Today, *Star Trek* is perhaps bigger and more mainstream than ever, with a succession of new series all running at the same time. Which is pretty good for a failed show that was taken off the air in 1969. And, inevitably, I've succumbed to the draw of the thing over the years—though I still have difficulty watching the remastered versions of the episodes that are common today. As crude and ridiculous and limited as the original effects footage was, I find that I like it better than the more polished, more plastic computer-generated special effects that have been substituted. Yes, they look better, but they don't look *better*, you know? But that's me all over, I suppose. I still don't love *Star Trek*.

Tom Brevoort is the VP of Publishing and Executive Editor of Marvel Comics, where he's worked as a part of the editorial team since 1989. Known unofficially as the "Master of the Marvel Arts," he's got an encyclopedic command of all things Marvel-related, a fact that drives him to write constantly about it and other aspects of the history of comics even when he isn't working. Guy should really get himself a hobby or something.

CAPTAIN'S LOG, STAR DATE: FOURTH GRADE

BY JOHN C. BRUENING

There's a lot about the sixties that I don't remember.

Yeah, I know. It sounds like a tired punchline to any number of tired jokes about the drug culture that was very much a part of that decade. But that's not what I'm getting at. My dim memory of the period has nothing to do with mind-altering substances, alcohol, or any of that. The reason I don't remember much about the sixties is because I was just too young.

But the boy who turned six at the end of 1969 has managed to hold onto a few dim but persistent memories.

In the America of the 1960s—for as troubled and troubling as things on the ground might have been, especially toward the end—our eyes were very much on a place beyond this world. We had committed ourselves to putting a man on the moon by the end of the decade and we had established a national space program that was prepared to do whatever it took to get there.

Because of this, space in the 1960s was no longer some inexplicable void beyond the Earth's atmosphere. By mid-decade, it was very much a part of our daily lives. The U.S. space program and the race against the Soviets to reach the moon had become part of the fabric of our Cold War culture. Astronauts in NASA's Mercury, Gemini and Apollo programs were celebrities. The names for various bits of rocket hardware had become part of the mainstream lexicon, and futuristic design elements had become a part of the furniture in our living rooms. Hell, the Ford Motor Company introduced an affordable family car called the Galaxie—and my parents had one parked in our driveway.

Perhaps the best part of all, space was on our TV screens.

Before I could work my way up to warp speed, I had to start slow. My earliest memory of space adventure on our black and white Zenith was actually that other group of intrepid explorers, the Robinson family. *Lost in Space* was ideal for a wide-eyed four- or five-year old. The show didn't ask too much of its viewers—especially in its second and third seasons, when the once-clever premise of a family in space morphed into something campy and absurd.

But that other show, the one on the other network. That was something altogether different. That was something for the big boys.

I wasn't even aware of *Star Trek* in its initial network run. I was not quite three years old when it premiered in September 1966 and five-and-a-half when the last episode aired in June 1969. If I had caught even the briefest glimpse of an episode in those first-run years, it would have been way past my level of comprehension. I didn't stumble upon the series until it was in syndicated reruns a couple years later in the early 1970s on one of Cleveland's two independent UHF stations—first the fledgling and short-lived Channel 61, and later (after 61 went dark) on Channel 43.

My first experience of the series came in bits in pieces. I'd catch five minutes of one episode here, ten minutes of another episode there. The language and the subject matter were extremely sophisticated, the characters were intelligent and multi-dimensional, the situations often felt deadly serious, and the starship on which many of the stories took place looked absolutely glorious. I remember my very young mind thinking, "I can't really grasp what's going on here, but this is just about the coolest thing I've ever seen on TV."

I barely understood the basic premise or the relationship between the main characters, but there were certain isolated scenes and scenarios that grabbed me, maybe even scared me a little, and stuck in my memory.

There was a rectangular machine, devoid of appendages, which called itself "Nomad" (many times) and somehow made its way onto the ship and moved up and down its corridors on its own power. It spoke to the crew in a flat but vaguely threatening voice, until the captain of the ship outsmarted it with a bit of inarguable logic that drove the voice into a high-pitched panic and forced the thing to blow a fuse.

There was a former officer, severely disabled and disfigured, no longer able to speak, confined to a futuristic wheelchair. He sat before some sort of review council and relived the events of a prior mission that involved an encounter with aliens who sported large, pulsating craniums and communicated without speaking.

There was the captain and his first officer, trapped in a place not of the future but clearly in the past—a soup kitchen in Depression-era America. They somehow had to fix the past in order to fix the future, but things got complicated when the captain developed a romantic entanglement with the attractive woman who ran the place.

Again, the captain and first officer, this time on a dark and murky planet, defying the warnings of a trio of nasty looking witches and wandering through what appeared to be a haunted castle. Inside, they narrowly avoid an attack by an enormous black cat, roughly the size of an elephant.

I mean, what? It was a hell of a lot, and probably too much, for an eight-year-old to process. But it was— to coin a phrase—fascinating.

And then a couple years later, somewhere around the fourth grade, along came Steven.

I probably don't have to say much to explain who or what he was. Everyone who ever attended elementary school or junior high knew a Steven. He was an anomaly, a misfit—a nerd before nerd status was fashionable. He was not at all athletic. He was socially awkward. He hadn't yet deciphered the social code—however rudimentary it is at that age—that would enable him to fit in, nor did he seem all that interested in figuring it out. But one thing was pretty clear, even by that early age: Steven operated at a different wavelength from the rest of us, on a cognitive plane that was significantly higher than any of his peers and even a few of his teachers. He was an enigma. And he was, not unlike those brief glimpses of random *Star Trek* episodes I'd caught here and there, fascinating.

Somehow, I wound up in Steven's orbit, for a little while at least.

Because, when all was said and done, I too was a bit of an anomaly and a misfit. I was skinny and uncoordinated and far from athletic. And I too struggled with the code. I wasn't as smart as Steven, but I knew there was something else going on beyond the narrow parameters of our hyper-structured Catholic grade school. Steven offered me at least a small window to what was on the other side.

I spent a few Saturdays at Steven's house, inside his world. It was a tightrope walk, because I wasn't ready to plunge completely down the rabbit hole without a tether or a trail of breadcrumbs to lead me back to the surface, but it was a pretty cool place to visit. He was into stuff that I was only vaguely aware of at the time. An elaborate game of fantasy and strategy called *Dungeons & Dragons*. An esoteric writer named J.R.R. Tolkien. A nationwide fascination with UFO sightings. (He was convinced that he'd once seen one himself.) And a prime-time science fiction TV series that had gone off the air just a few years earlier but was readily available in syndication every weeknight on the ultra-high frequencies of the broadcast spectrum.

Star Trek.

He had seen every episode, knew every one of them by its title. He could summarize every plot in just a sentence or two.

"What's the episode about the talking metal box called Nomad?"

"'The Changeling.'"

"How about the guy in the wheelchair with the scarred face?"

"'The Menagerie.'"

"What's the one that takes place in a Depression-era soup kitchen?"

"'The City on the Edge of Forever.'"

"What about the one with the three witches and the giant cat?"

"'Cat's Paw.'"

Steven knew them. He knew them all.

He lent me a book called *The Making of Star Trek*, written by Stephen Whitfield and series creator Gene Roddenberry and published in 1968, when the show was still in its original prime-time run—after the famous fan letter campaign that convinced the network to keep it on the air for a third season. So now I not only had a friend who could help me make sense of the episodes themselves, I had a book that took me behind the scenes and showed me how the series was conceived and how it got on the air every week less than a decade earlier.

And that's when it all finally got into high gear for me. I went home and started watching the reruns—in their entirety for the first time, beginning to end, every weeknight on Channel 43.

The adventures were certainly perilous and entertaining, but I realized pretty quickly that there was something else going on under the surface. For every alien menace and sleek bit of 23rd-century gadgetry deployed to confront it, there was also a very human component to every story (and I use the word "human" loosely in this context). At the heart of all the intergalactic drama were thought-provoking questions about logic and reason versus ignorance, cultural harmony versus prejudice and disunity, diplomacy versus violence, and the perseverance of humanity amid the march of technology.

But the thing that attracted me even more—and still does to this day—was the chemistry of the recurring characters: A youthful and unflinching starship captain, full of piss and vinegar and possessed of a spine made of pure steel. A stoic first officer, not of this world and seemingly devoid of emotion, with a razor-sharp intellect that often proved to be a powerful weapon. A curmudgeonly medical officer, whose assessment of himself as "a simple country doctor" belied his true abilities as a gifted healer. A Black female communication officer. (Read that again: A Black female officer. Sitting just over the captain's right shoulder in a command center otherwise populated by men. In 1965.) A Scotsman in the engine room. An Asian navigator. A Russian helmsman.

The crew of the USS *Enterprise* was as magnificent looking as the ship itself, a mosaic of the best that this or any other world had to offer.

I certainly wasn't the first person to notice all this. Even at the time of the series' initial network run, members of the scientific community—many of the same people who were working on getting American astronauts to the moon—recognized *Star Trek* for the groundbreaking slice of pop culture entertainment that it was.

Roddenberry was doing something unheard of, going boldly where no television creator had gone before and dressing up his handiwork in a futuristic and adventurous setting that made it safe for prime time. And in syndicated reruns just a few years later, it was still an enlightening experience for this fifth grader.

By the time I finished grade school a couple years later, I had seen just about every episode at least once. The idea of full TV series collections on VHS tape was still a few years off, so I had to navigate the occasionally erratic shuffle of Channel 43's programming schedule to fill in the random episode that I might have missed here or there. I can't say I was a died-in-the-wool Trekker by the time I was fourteen, but the original *Star Trek* series had gotten under my skin in a way that I had yet to realize over the next few decades.

After grade school, Steven and I headed in different directions and lost touch. I had climbed back up the tether, back to the surface, where high school and eventually college were right around the corner and things like rock and roll and girls were looking more and more appealing by the day. Had I been braver, maybe I would have stayed in his world a little longer and embraced more of it. But there was that adage about becoming a man and putting away childish things. (Which is a trap, by the way. It took me decades to figure that out, but I've been a lot more settled with myself since I did. And that's another discussion for another time.)

The good news is that I held onto some of what he showed me. I never took the plunge into *Dungeons & Dragons*, but I still have the same Tolkien books I bought in the '70s. I'm still mildly intrigued by accounts of UFO sightings, even the ones that have been long since debunked. And I'm still drawn to those original 79 episodes of *Star Trek*.

The franchise has since been reinvented and spun off nearly a dozen times, on small screens and big ones. In the process, it has become an industry unto itself. I've dialed in to some of the various iterations for a brief glimpse, and it all has a certain undeniable appeal—artistically as well as technically—but none of it has had that same holy-god-I-can't-even-comprehend-what-I'm-seeing-but-

I-can't-look-away effect on me. That's the kind of experience you only get when you're ten or twelve years old and the world is still an unexplored galaxy. Once you transition out of that chapter of your life, it's very hard to go back.

But every once in a while, I'll stream an episode or two of the original series. When I do, I might chuckle a little bit at William Shatner's occasionally ham-fisted portrayal of the blustery Captain James T. Kirk. Or the alien terrains littered with boulders that are obviously nothing more than carefully painted lumps of Styrofoam scattered across a sound stage. Or the creaky special visual effects that predate CGI technology by at least a couple decades. Or the predictable fate of nearly every red-shirted crew member who appears on camera. Or the number of times Dr. Leonard "Bones" McCoy examines a body in the first act and informs his commanding officer in his grim and raspy voice, "He's dead Jim…"

But if I do chuckle, it's only for a moment or two. It's easy to look past all that stuff when you can see what Roddenberry was aiming for, the bigger picture he was trying to paint, the greater story he was trying to tell. After the first few minutes, more than fifty years later, I'm inevitably back on the five-year mission, once again going as boldly as I can.

And it's still fascinating.

At various times since the 1980s, **John C. Bruening** has worked as a journalist, newspaper and magazine editor, marketing specialist, novelist, short story writer and essayist. He is a co-founder and editor at Flinch Books, the publisher of his 2016 debut novel, *The Midnight Guardian: Hour of Darkness*. The Midnight Guardian series has since continued with *Annihilation Machine* (2019) and *God and Sinners* (2022). He has also written numerous short stories and essays for anthologies published by Becky Books, Stormgate Press, Moonstone Books, Blue Planet Press and others. He lives with his wife Mariah in a suburb of Cleveland, Ohio (and sometimes their two children live with them when they're not away at college and preparing to take on the world).

TO BOLDY GO

BY RON HILL

IT WAS NOVEMBER, 1968... I WAS SLEEPING OVER AT GRANDMA AND GRANDPA HILL'S HOUSE IN ROCKY RIVER, OHIO.

AFTER A BURGER AT BOB'S BIG BOY, I WAS DRAWING, AS USUAL.

INSTEAD OF GOLF OR AN INDIANS GAME, GRANDPA WAS WATCHING SOMETHING, WELL...*DIFFERENT*.

SUDDENLY, I WAS DRAWN TO THE TV SCREEN BY A STRANGE "WHOOSH" AND A GUY TALKING...

...TO BOLDLY GO...

THESE THREE GUYS IN BLUE AND GOLD SHIRTS APPEARED OUT OF NOWEHERE.
AND ONE GUY'S EARS WERE POINTY!
THEY REMINDED ME OF MINE - I WAS GETTING PICKED ON AT SCHOOL, KIDS CALLING ME "RABBIT EARS."
I DON'T KNOW IF GRANDPA HAD SEEN THIS SHOW BEFORE, BUT I SURE HADN'T.

I DIDN'T GET THE SPOOKY MIND-CONTROL THING THAT WAS GOING ON IN ONE PART.

I DID RECOGNIZE ONE GUY FROM "WILD WILD WEST," A SHOW MOM THOUGHT WAS TOO VIOLENT...

...AND THE CAPTAIN WAS NICE, BUT TOUGH, A LOT LIKE JIM WEST.

I REMEMBER COVERING MY EYES AT THE MUSHY KISSING SCENE!

BUT I PEEKED.

Ron Hill has drawn for *Dungeons & Dragons* games, illustrated Presbyterian Publishing Company's Armchair Theologian series, been sued (unsuccessfully) for defamation by a notoriously litigious coal magnate, and has been writing and drawing tens of thousands of editorial cartoons, comic strips, illustrations, and caricatures since the mid-1970s. In June 2023, his documentary film, *Go-kart Therapy*, was invited to screen at the 14th Annual Chagrin Documentary Film Festival in October of that year. He is currently directing *We Are Doc Savage: A Documentary on Fandom*. Learn more at RonHillArtist.com.

SCARE TREK

BY GREG COX

I honestly can't remember when I wasn't a Trekkie—and a Monster Kid. I can credit my dad for both of those. Just as he let me stay up past my bedtime to watch *Star Trek* with him during its original run on NBC, he also exposed me to its immediate predecessors, *The Twilight Zone* and *The Outer Limits*, as well as classic monster movies like *Godzilla* and *The Fly* and *The Creature from the Black Lagoon*, which were already airing on TV by the time I was growing up in the neutral zone between Seattle and Tacoma, Washington. Dad loved scary stuff, having grown up on the original black-and-white Universal Monster movies, *The Shadow* and *Inner Sanctum* on the radio, and *Tales from the Crypt* comics in his teens, and he passed that taste for having one's spine deliciously tingled onto me, along with introducing me to this cool new sci-fi show titled *Star Trek*, which ended up being rerun perpetually in syndication for the rest of my childhood and adolescence.

And here's the thing: being a first-generation Trekkie *and* a died-in-the-wool Monster Kid overlapped in a big way. Nowadays much is made of the fact that *Star Trek* presented an almost uniquely optimistic vision of a future one would actually want to live in, and that's absolutely a fundamental part of its appeal, but I would be lying if I didn't admit that, as a kid, I was also tuning into Trek for the unearthly thrills and chills awaiting unwary redshirts out on the Final Frontier.

And, yes, for the monsters, too.

Nor should this be too surprising in the context of the times. As noted, my experience with SF media back then came mostly from movies like *Mothra* and *The Blob* and *The Amazing Colossal Man* and, as noted, tv shows like *The Twilight Zone* and *The Outer Limits*, all of which could get pretty scary at times. Long before the latter-day

Trek shows came along, these productions were what shaped my expectations regarding the original *Star Trek* TV series which, honestly, owes more to *TZ* and *Outer Limits* than modern-day Trekkies may appreciate. Like *TZ*, *Star Trek* was fond of ironic twist endings: the scary alien is actually a futuristic scarecrow, or a protective mother, or a bratty child, or a pair of spindly, fragile creatures who looked like they were made out of pipe cleaners. And like *Outer Limits*, which proudly displayed a grotesque new creature every episode[14], *Trek* was not shy about occasionally playing the monster card to keep us sixties and seventies kids glued to the screen: the Salt Vampire, the Gorn, the Mugato, giant spear-throwing ape-men, flying neural parasites, killer androids, and even the voracious spirit of Jack the Ripper. Meanwhile, as far as young Greg was concerned, *Star Trek*, in both its original run and subsequent syndication, also overlapped with *Dark Shadows* (1966-1971) and, locally, with *Nightmare Theatre*, our regional late-night horror-movie showcase, which provided me with a thorough education in vintage sci-fi and monster movies, which were often pretty much one and the same, featuring monsters and menaces born of mad science, atomic radiation, and the ominous mysteries of outer space.

In short, as a child of the sixties, I had every reason to expect and hope that *Star Trek* would sometimes scare me as much as *Twilight Zone* and *The Outer Limits* and the likes of *Tarantula* and *Monster on the Campus* did—and I was not disappointed.

Herewith, my own personal log of some of *Star Trek*'s scariest moments:

"Charlie X": Is there any moment more disturbing in the *Enterprise*'s original five-year mission than that brief glimpse of some poor unnamed crewwoman stumbling blindly around a corner after having her face literally erased by Charlie Evan's telekinetic powers? Her features instantly replaced by a flesh-colored blank, she's lost her eyes, her nose, her mouth, her identity, maybe even her life. *How can she breathe?* I wondered anxiously as a kid, and I worry about that still. The episode ends with the godlike Thasians assuring Kirk that they've repaired whatever damage Charlie's done to

---

[14]This is where I cop to collecting *Outer Limits* bubble gum cards as a kid, with a new and different monster on every card!

the ship and crew, but I'm not sure I bought that, then or now. We never do find out what happened to the Faceless Woman or see her restored, and that lack of closure only makes her brief appearance all the more troubling.

"The Squire of Gothos": Dare I admit that this episode literally gave me nightmares? "Seriously?" I hear you ask. "A foppish Liberace wannabe, who turns out to be nothing more than a petulant little boy, actually scared you? Just how wimpy a kid were you, Greg?"

But go back and watch the final act of the episode. Sure, Trelane seems more ridiculous than menacing at first, but he becomes steadily more malevolent as Kirk and crew fail to show him the admiration he feels he deserves, ultimately becoming genuinely murderous. Now consider Kirk's situation at the end: cut off from his crew, confined to the only patch of breathable atmosphere on a planet otherwise inhospitable to human life, being hunted for sport by a sadistic being with seemingly godlike powers…and then that hangman's noose materializes out of nowhere.

Tell me that's not nightmare fuel!

"The Devil in the Dark": Sure, sure, we find out eventually that the mass-murdering Horta is really just a grief-stricken mother desperate to protect her eggs, and certainly the episode ends on an upbeat note with humans and Hortas learning to live together in a mutually beneficial arrangement. It's all very heart-warming and inspirational and one of my all-time favorite TOS episodes[15].

Yet *before* we get to that well-earned happy ending, we get horrific scenes of frightened men being burned alive by a scuttling, cave-dwelling creature that (Spock takes pains to explain) secretes a *highly* corrosive acid that burns through solid rock as easily as it reduces living flesh and bone to ashes. We see the steaming, incinerated remains of the Horta's victims, as well as the terror of their final moments, and it's pretty obvious that, regardless of the creature's motives, death by Horta acid is not exactly a pleasant way to go.

Acid has always creeped me out to an inordinate degree, possibly from seeing Claude Rains' face scorched by acid in *The Phantom of the Opera* (1943) at an impressionable age, so a creature that secretes

---

[15]Shameless plug: My first professional Star Trek novel, co-authored with John Gregory Betancourt, was a semi-sequel to this ep titled *Devil in the Sky*.

a super-powerful acid from its very pores was yet more nightmare fodder. And, honestly, it wasn't just the Horta herself that scared me; I got the willies every time Kirk and Spock explored some freshly-burrowed tunnel whose edges were still steaming from the Horta's passage. *Watch out! Don't touch the edges! Don't get any acid on you!* I'd mentally warn Kirk, who was way too recklessly eager to venture into those newly-formed tunnels for my peace of mind. Would it have killed him to put on some rubber gloves first just in case the acid hadn't all steamed away yet? Safety first!

And then Spock had to actually *touch* the Horta to communicate with it?

Talk about nerve-wracking!

"What are Little Girls Made Of?": I'd like to say that I knew who Robert Bloch was when I first watched (and rewatched) this episode as a kid, but, like a Vulcan, I cannot tell a lie, supposedly. But even without realizing that Bloch was a legendary horror writer, best known for writing the novel that inspired Hitchcock's *Psycho*, the horror-movie vibe came through loud and clear. You had *Lurch* menacing Kirk for Charles Addams' sake, in the form of a looming, homicidal android you definitely didn't want to run into a dark alien cavern.

But, as monstrous as Ruk the killer android was, with his cadaverous features and bottomless, sepulchral voice, even as ferocious as he was during his final rampage ("That is the equation! Existence!"), Ruk is *not* the most disturbing thing in the episode: that's the chilling moment when scientist Roger Korby is revealed to be an android who only thinks he's the real Korby, at least in every way that matters. The scene where he tries and fails to convince his horrified fiancée, Christine Chapel, that he's still the same person despite having transferred his consciousness into a soulless, coldly logical android body is genuinely unnerving, as is Kirk's grim assessment of the situation: "Doctor Korby was never here."

For some reason, the idea of being turned into a robot, and losing my own identity in the process, really got under my skin when I was a kid. I remember being similarly freaked out by a long-ago episode of *Lost in Space* in which some kind of alien conveyor belt turned young Will Robinson into a robotic duplicate of Dr. Smith. I was never into *Lost in Space* the way I was with *Star Trek* and have largely forgotten whatever episodes of the show I inevitably watched back then, but the ghastly visual of Will transformed, mentally and physically, into a pint-sized Dr. Smith still makes me shudder, even close to sixty years later.

Just like the artificial Korby did.

"Wolf in the Fold": Robert Bloch strikes again, although this would have still flown over my head the first few times I watched this one. It wasn't until I was twelve years old and picked up a certain Marvel horror comic at our local 7-Eleven[16], featuring a comics adaptation of Bloch's classic 1943 short story "Yours Truly, Jack the Ripper," that I fully grasped that Bloch had recycled the same basic idea—that Jack the Ripper was an immortal entity killing endlessly across time—as another memorably creepy *Star Trek* episode!

But Jack the Ripper meets *Star Trek*, with death lurking in dimly-lit alleys suffused with swirling dry-ice fog straight out of a vintage Universal Monster flick? And an eerie séance that ends with yet hair-raising death? "Wolf in the Fold" gave me the sci-fi futurism of *Star Trek* mixed with classic old-school horror tropes.

What more could a Trekkie/Monster Kid want?

And then there's "Catspaw," *Star Trek*'s one-and-only Halloween episode, originally airing on October 27, 1967, when I was only seven years old. Nowadays "Catspaw" does not generally enjoy a good reputation among *Trek* fans, so that admitting to liking "Catspaw" is definitely a minority position, but growing up I was always excited when it would turn up in the rotation of the syndicated reruns, for much the same reason that I eagerly looked forward to the occasional random showings of the vampire episode of *Gilligan's Island*. I loved it because it combined two of my favorite things—*Star Trek* and Halloween—in one delicious package, complete with witches, a haunted castle, a medieval dungeon (with decorative skeleton), more swirling fog, and even a giant black cat worthy of a 1950s drive-in horror movie. It was the Reese's Peanut Cup of *Trek* episodes: two great tastes that taste great together.

[16] *Journey Into Mystery* #2 (December 1972), to be precise.

And, yes, it was written by Bloch as well.

"A Taste for Armageddon": On the surface, this thought-provoking, high-concept SF piece about the pros and cons of virtual warfare conducted entirely by linked computers lacks the sort of visceral shocks and scares found in more overtly horrific *Trek* episodes. No redshirts die, violently or otherwise. There are no grotesque alien beings or monsters. As with the bloodless war being waged by the two rival planets, the dangers are purely abstract—until you're required to promptly report to the nearest convenient disintegration chamber because a computer has declared you a fatality of an imaginary "attack." Suicide as a civic duty.

Is it just me or is the very *idea* of ordinary, law-abiding citizens voluntarily lining up to be disintegrated enough to send a chill down your spine? As a generally responsible, well-behaved child who was perhaps overly inclined to follow the rules, do my homework, and not cause a fuss, I couldn't help wondering what I would do if I was asked to step into one of those chambers, especially if I'd been taught my entire life that this was a necessary sacrifice for the good of society, expected of all decent, patriotic men, women, and children? Would peer pressure and a sense of duty be enough to make me meekly submit to my own execution, like a lamb to a slaughter? Or more to the point, like the docile Eloi marching blithely into the maw of the cannibalistic Morlocks in the classic 1960 movie version of *The Time Machine?*

To be honest, I genuinely can't remember if I saw "A Taste of Armageddon" before or after I watched *The Time Machine* on TV for the first time, but I would have been exposed to both of them around the same age, thanks to my dad, and that same basic idea—of ordinary people passively consenting to their own destruction because they didn't know any better – frightened me both times.

And speaking of disintegration, how about the transporters anyway? Sure, I appreciated the convenience of being able to beam down a planet instead of having to land a shuttlecraft every time you visited some strange new world, but…getting taken apart, atom by atom, and then reassembled somewhere else, hopefully all in one piece? Trust me, Doctor McCoy wasn't the only one who found that prospect somewhat unsettling. I'd seen *The Fly* (the original with Vincent Price, not the remake), so knew just how horribly things could go wrong when you start messing around with teleportation.

Indeed, growing up, I was utterly convinced that *Star Trek*'s transporters were based on the pioneering work of David Hedison in *The Fly*, and I used to worry about a fly or some other tiny organism getting into the same transporter beam as Captain Kirk.

For the love of God, why were there no No-Pest Strips in the transporter room?

These are just a sample of *Star Trek*'s eerier moments and episodes, the ones that personally gave me the creeps as a kid. I could've just as easily cited the alien-possession shudders of "The Lights of Zetar," especially when the titular Lights garble the speech of one poor woman right before she expires, or the swarms of flying neural parasites swooping in inflict agonizing deaths on their victims in "Operation—Annihilate!," or even the demonic blood-red Spinning Pinwheel of Hate that feeds vampirically on the destructive enmity between humans and Klingons in "Day of the Dove," but…you get the idea. For all the hope and optimism offered by *Star Trek*'s positive vision of the future, the horror fan in me was also a sucker for those special occasions when Trek went boldly beyond the outer limits to a twilight zone of strange new nightmares and monsters.

Trick or treat!

Greg Cox has been a professional Trekkie for more than thirty years. He is the *New York Times* bestselling author of numerous *Star Trek* novels and short stories, including *The Black Shore, Assignment: Eternity, The Q Continuum* trilogy, *The Eugenics Wars (Volumes One and Two), The Rings of Time, Foul Deeds Will Rise, The Weight of Worlds, No Time Like the Past, Child of Two Worlds, Legacies: Captain to Captain, The Antares Maelstrom,* and *A Contest of Principles.* He has received six Scribe Awards, including one for Life Achievement, from the International Association of Media Tie-In Writers. Visit him at: www.gregcox-author.com.

AND THE CHILD SHALL TREK FOREVER MORE

BY DAYTON WARD

It's a typical afternoon in Tampa, Florida, circa 1978. I'm eleven years old and I've just walked home from school. I let myself in because I'm one of those "latchkey kids" with my own house key. Since both my parents work and my sister is on a different school schedule which won't see her home for another hour or so, I've got the place to myself but there are also things to be done. Let the dog out. Pull something from the freezer to defrost for dinner. It's not the day I usually cut the grass, and I've checked the pool to make sure it doesn't need skimming or cleaning. With those tasks accomplished, I settle in at the dining room table and start in on my homework. In our house, the television is off limits until homework and chores are finished. However, my sister and I are allowed a single exception to that rule, as we each have a favorite program.

For me, it's *Star Trek*.

Given the overall theme connecting the entries in this volume, that probably shouldn't be a surprise. What I didn't know during those very early days—what I could not possibly imagine at that time—was just how much *Star Trek* would ultimately change the course of my life.

Its influence actually began several years earlier. I was born while the series was in production, but I didn't discover it until those daily reruns of the original series on a local UHF station, with additional episodes on Saturdays during certain times of the year. Saturday viewings were usually accompanied by episodes of other 1960s science fiction TV staples such as *Lost In Space* and *Voyage to the Bottom of the Sea*. This ritual began sometime in 1972 or so while we lived on

Long Island, New York. Once I started school, I was able to catch the daily rerun in the early afternoon before my father returned home from work and commandeered the living room television to watch the news or perhaps a baseball game. This relegated me along with the adventures of the U.S.S. *Enterprise* to the little black and white TV my parents let me have in my bedroom.

Watching those daily reruns, I thought Captain Kirk was a brave, inspiring leader, and if we're being honest, he remains a childhood hero for me, a boy who grew into a man while still retaining a bit of that kid at heart. Meanwhile, Spock was super cool with that thing he kept calling a "computer," inspiring me to take classes and eventually forge a career as a software developer that lasted nearly thirty years.

I'm often asked about my favorite episodes of the show. Do I have a list? A "Top 10?" The answer is yes, but it's a soft yes. As a kid, I held in high regard what I suspect are common favorites: "Balance of Terror," "The Menagerie," "Arena," "Space Seed," "The City on the Edge of Forever," "Mirror, Mirror," "The Doomsday Machine," and "The Tholian Web," but also less-common picks like "Tomorrow Is Yesterday," "Court-Martial," and "Assignment: Earth." Heck, I'm still waiting for that *Assignment: Earth* spin-off series.

Long before I grew old enough to understand that these episodes possessed layers and subtle (and not-so subtle) messages and themes baked into their stories, I simply loved them for their action-adventure elements, with Kirk and his crew doing brave deeds to save the day from this or that threat. Also, who doesn't like to see Kirk throwing down with Khan, the Gorn, Wyatt Earp, an Orion disguised as an Andorian, or even his best buddy Spock? So enamored was I with all the crazy fight scenes that decades later it would compel me to write the official book on how to fight just like Captain Kirk. Consult your local bookseller for all the crazy details!

Of course, as I grew older, I began to understand those episodes on whole new levels. That it's nearly sixty years since the show premiered and I can still find something new to appreciate from it is a testament to the quality of its storytelling and how easily it can draw me back to enjoy it all over again.

Meanwhile, back in the early 1970s, my father usually worked on Saturday mornings, which often meant I could grab a bowl of cereal and plop down on the living room rug to watch cartoons. On September 8, 1973, it was this practice which allowed me to watch "Beyond the Farthest Star," a *Star Trek* episode I'd never seen before and the premiere installment of the animated offshoot which served as an extension of those reruns I'd been consuming most days to that point. Yes, it was a "cartoon" (though we don't really call it that, do we?), but even at that young age I could tell this was something altogether different from something like *Speed Buggy* or *Super Friends*, both of which just so happened to premiere on that same Saturday morning. I heard the familiar voices of William Shatner, Leonard Nimoy, and (most of) the original series cast, and there was the *Enterprise* sailing through animated space. Even the opening credits seemed oddly familiar, accompanied by an inversion of every note from the original show's iconic main theme. Between this and the weekday reruns of the live-action series, I was set for *Star Trek*, right?

Wrong.

As it happens, those glimpses into the final frontier via my television screen were just the figurative tip of the proverbial iceberg.

I don't recall with absolute certainty, but I'm confident one of the first model kits I ever assembled—if not *the* first—was the U.S.S. *Enterprise* produced by Aluminum Model Toys. AMT had been producing the model for several years by the time I got my grubby little paws on one. I was probably eight years old when I put one of these together for the first time, complete with shoddy paint job and marginally well-placed decals. I'm pretty sure I had it for a month or so before I took it outside to run around while holding it aloft and making what I thought were passable imitations of warp drive sounds. Then I dropped it on the sidewalk, breaking it far beyond my limited ability to repair.

Then I used my allowance to buy another one, so I could go through all of that again. I'd like to think the paint and decals came out better on this second attempt, and my skill would continue to improve as I acquired additional replacements for subsequent kits which suffered fates similar to that first model.

Hey, childhood playtime used to be pretty hazardous.

While I didn't build all of the *Star Trek* models AMT produced, I did assemble the *Galileo* shuttlecraft, the *Enterprise* bridge diorama, and the "Exploration Set" with its fun-size, less than *exactly* screen-accurate yet still totally cool phaser, communicator, and tricorder. That last kit? Yeah, I ended up playing with those outside, too. Guess what happened to them?

Then there were the actual toys. Mego, one of the more prolific providers of action figures in the early to mid-1970s, had among its various licensed offerings a range of figures based on *Star Trek*. Captain Kirk, Mr. Spock, Dr. McCoy, Scotty, and Lieutenant Uhura represented "the good guys," and with the notable exception of Uhura bore fairly accurate likenesses of the actors in something of a blending of their live-action and animated countenances. This was more than enough for young Dayton, who used these figures to create his own *Star Trek* adventures. These improvised sagas, carried out on the floor of my bedroom or our living room, often included guest starring roles for the likes of Batman, Superman, General Urko and others from *Planet of the Apes*, G.I. Joe, and—of course—The Six Million Dollar Man himself, Steve Austin with his see-through eye and "bionic arm."

(It's entirely possible I've continued to carry out comparable simulations as an adult, though I disguise my motives by claiming to choreograph fight scenes for a story I'm writing.)

The success of the original line of *Star Trek* figures along with Mego's delightfully inaccurate yet still oddly charming "U.S.S. *Enterprise* Action Playset" saw to it that more figures were needed. The initial villainous offering, the "Klingon," was soon joined in my toybox by a follow-up line of "Aliens." Eight figures were released in two waves of four, and each bore varying degrees of passing resemblance to actual aliens seen on the TV show. Among these, the "Mugato" and the "Talosian" are the most outrageously inaccurate of the figures, and absolutely by favorites of the bunch. The one item

I longed for but never got? That insane "Mission to Gamma VI" playset with the faux Vaal edifice from "The Apple." Just as many Star Wars fans of my generation still hunt for Kenner's amazing 1978 "Death Star Space Station" playset while willing to settle for one in anything resembling decent condition, so it is with me and "Mission to Gamma VI." You know, in case anyone reading this is stumped on what to get me for my birthday. Barring that? I keep a kidney on standby for special occasions.

Also, and since the statute of limitations is long past, I have a confession to make to dear Mrs. Walters who lived two doors down from us: Even though I blamed it on that I kid I didn't like across the street, it was in fact me who strapped a well-worn Captain Kirk figure—who at that point was missing an arm as a consequence of overly-rough handling—to a model rocket which caught fire as it launched from the quad in front of our townhomes before quickly plummeting back to Earth to be consumed by fire on your lawn. Sorry.

Speaking of playing outside, younger readers might not believe this, but it was an actual thing back in the "Before Time." You know, the era before personal computers, cell phones, the internet and streaming, cable TV, and even VCRs let alone DVD or Blu-ray players. Should I even mention LaserDisc players? Okay, I will, but only so that I can say the Before Time was before those, too. It's fair to say if any of that existed for the home market in 1975 or so, I'd have succumbed to its sweet, sweet embrace. Even if it did, we weren't all that rich, so fun was where we found it and what we made of it.

For me and my friends, that meant "playing" *Star Trek*.

Not just with those aforementioned action figures and playsets, you understand, but heading outside to explore strangely familiar areas of our neighborhood, playing *Star Trek* the way we might have played "Cowboys and Indians" or "Army." We had our Mego communicator walkie-talkies and our "Tracer Guns" with those little plastic discs you could use against your friends in the days before worrying about shooting your buddy's eye out was a thing.

(We're not even going to talk about the "first generation" of *Star*

Trek toys from Remco, which is to say toys made for something else and slapped with a semi-sorta almost-but-not-quite *Star Trek* logo. On the other hand, the delightfully wacky "*Star Trek* Space Fun Helmet" produced by Enco Industries is something I still covet to this day. Again, I've got this extra kidney just doing nothing but waiting for a good excuse to donate it.)

One of us might have had the nifty "Super Phaser II Target Game" phaser, or the smaller version from that AMT Exploration Set model kit. Or maybe just a stick, because we were poor and imagination filled in all the blanks, anyway. That big crazy metal ball with the slides and ladders at the center of the local playground, which might even cook you alive on a summer day if it got hot enough? That was our Starship *Enterprise* (and, for a short time, Moonbase Alpha from *Space: 1999*). Some of us played Captain Kirk or Spock or other characters we made up, and others played the Klingons.

In and around all of this, and with increasing frequency as I got a bit older, another dimension was added to by nascent *Star Trek* fandom: Reading. As a kid in the 1970s, finding *Star Trek* stories on the printed page was something of a challenge. There were the comics from Gold Key, published on a rather erratic schedule and available only as the odd issues I might find at the local drug or department store, as I wouldn't even learn comic bookstores were a thing until the mid-1980s. If you're reading this, then you know those old Gold Key comics were not exactly a faithful representation of Captain Kirk and his crew from the TV series. The stories were pretty simplistic, and accurate so far as ships and equipment left much to be desired. I mean, are we really hoping one of the current *Star Trek* television series introduces the pink backpacks and rifles or shows us flames blasting from the rear of the *Enterprise*'s warp nacelles (or its shuttlecraft hangar bay doors, if we're feeling froggy)? And yet, despite their truly hilarious quirks, they like some of the toys and models hold an unassailable charm for me. They are an intrinsic part of my *Star Trek* experience in those days.

Then there were the paperback books. My journey to *Star Trek* stories in novel form came from those classic adaptations of original series episodes as penned by noted science fiction author James Blish. The first paperback book I bought with my own money was Blish's *Star Trek 4*. Here was a way to relive favorite episodes from my favorite TV show, and what do you know? There were eleven more books just like this one! Bantam Books, who published the Blish novelizations, also produced over a dozen novels and two short story collections between 1968 and 1980, the latter portion of that period being my *Star Trek* childhood sweet spot.

I still recall the day my mother, volunteering for the Scholastic book fair at my elementary school, brought home for me a copy of *Star Trek 5* and *The Enterprise Logs* Volume 2, a collection of Gold Key comics in the days well before "trade paperback collection" became a comic industry mainstay. In many ways, I owe my mother a good portion of credit for the weird *Star Trek* curve my life eventually ended up taking. Even though she never understood my love for the show, she indulged me this particular early passion of mine, making sure I had that extra dollar I needed to buy that new *Star Trek* book or maybe even the latest issue of the wonderful *Star Trek Giant Poster Book*, in actuality a magazine you opened (then opened again, then opened *again*) to reveal a new poster for your bedroom wall.

(Sorry, Spock. You eventually got replaced by Farrah Fawcett, but we'll talk about that in another essay for another book. Maybe.)

During this same period, another publisher, Ballantine Books, produced a series of similar efforts for the animated series as provided by author Alan Dean Foster. Then came 1979 and something of a quantum shift for *Star Trek* on the printed page, as Simon & Schuster through its Pocket Books imprint acquired a license to publish *Star Trek* novels beginning with an adaptation of the script for *Star Trek: The Motion Picture* as penned by the Great Bird of the Galaxy himself, Gene Roddenberry. As I write this, S&S continues to publish *Star Trek* novels to this day, with a backlist numbering more than six hundred novels along with a multitude of novellas, short story collections, and reference books. Reading *Star Trek* stories in book form also introduced me to the wider science fiction genre. I started out with the names you might expect: Clarke, Matheson, Asimov, Bradbury, Heinlein. Those writers of yesteryear created stories I still love to this day, along with more recent voices like Baxter, Scalzi, Unger, and Weir to name just a few.

And here's that curveball from Mom I hinted at earlier: Little did I know that my love for reading *Star Trek* fiction, fueled in large part by the ongoing publishing efforts but also those early indulgences on my mother's part, would one day lead me to writing and publishing *Star Trek* fiction of my own for S&S, something I've been doing on a regular basis for twenty-five years. And yes, creating new stories for Captain Kirk and the crew of the original *Enterprise* is still one of my very favorite things to write. Thanks, Mom.

Today, *Star Trek* is everywhere. It's on our TVs, on our shelves, and even in our pockets if you want to watch an episode on your phone. The original series (and all of the spinoffs, but we're keeping things on theme here) is available on-demand via streaming or home media. And yet, one of my favorite ways to revisit the show is catching the odd episode on MeTV, the over-the-air broadcast network specializing in classic television shows from years and decades past. The original *Star Trek* is a staple of their lineup, and watching an episode there—commercial breaks, savage editing, and all—can instantly transport me back to that 1970s living room rug with a smile on my face.

Oh, and I still want that "Mission to Gamma VI" set. And the Space Fun Helmet.

Dayton Ward is a *New York Times* bestselling author or co-author of more than forty novels and novellas, often working with his best friend, Kevin Dilmore. His short fiction has appeared in more than thirty anthologies, and he's written for magazines such as *NCO Journal, Kansas City Voices, Famous Monsters of Filmland, Star Trek* and *Star Trek Communicator* as well as the websites Tor.com, Star-Trek.com, and Syfy.com. And yes, he really did write the official book on how to fight like Captain Kirk. Check out *Star Trek: Kirk Fu*, wherever you buy your books. Learn more about Dayton and his writing at daytonward.com.

A VOICE IN THE WILDERNESS

BY VAN ALLEN PLEXICO

I had beamed down alone to this weird planet covered in what looked like ancient ruins. Since nobody was around, I started talking to myself as I took some tricorder readings. The very first thing I said out loud, randomly, was: "I wonder what TV series had the greatest special effects in television history?"

And then this weird voice boomed out:

"A question! Since before your sun burned hot in space, and before your race was born, I have awaited a question."

"Ahh! Look out! It's a giant flat doughnut that flashes lights, emits smoke, and talks!"

"Yes. Though that is a poor description of me. I am better known as… (dramatic pause) *…the Guardian of Forever!"*

"Okay, yeah. I've heard of you."

"Then speak your question, human!"

"Ummm… What was I asking, again? Oh yeah. Which television series had the best special effects ever?"

(More flashing lights; more smoke.)

"The answer, of course, is subjective. Viewers perceive such things differently. What appears amazing to one seems amateurish to another."

"Ahh, you're prevaricating, giant smoky doughnut. Answer the question!"

(Still more flashing and more smoke.)

"For you, Van Allen Plexico, there is only one answer. And the answer is: Star Trek.*"*

"*Star Trek*? You mean like *Discovery*? Or *Picard*? One of these shows on Paramount Plus, with a big budget and all the sophisticated CGI effects and—"

"No, I mean Star Trek.*"*

(A long pause.)

*"*What? Just *regular Star Trek?* The Original Series, as it's called now? How can that be? That series was produced on an increasingly diminishing budget, way back in the Sixties! You can practically see the wires holding the ships up!*"*

"Today you can, yes. But, back then, you—you, Van Allen Plexico—couldn't. And therein lies the beginning of the answer."

*"*Wait...*What?"*

(*Lots* of smoke and flashing.)

"For the answer to make sense to you, and to the reader, we must travel back... back into what was. Back into the mists of the past."

"Uh oh."

(Yeah, the smoke is really pouring out of that big doughnut now!)

"Step through the portal that is the Guardian of Forever and witness the bizarre and remote vista that was...Alabama in the Seventies!"

"Oh jeez."

(Spooky transition effects.)

(In slow motion, Van steps out of an invisible portal and into a small, two-bedroom house with plywood paneling and white foam drop-ceiling. A big, boxy Zenith color TV stands in the corner, the screen black. An elderly woman fiddles around in the kitchen to the left.)

"Alabama. The Seventies. Yep—here we are..."

Yes, here we are, indeed. Smack-dab in the middle of nowhere, many miles from the nearest town. Far out in the countryside beyond Sylacauga, Alabama. It's probably 1976, and I'm a second-grader, arriving home from school.

I live with my grandparents, but they're both in their seventies and have little time for me and no interest in (and less patience for) what I enjoy most: science fiction TV shows, books and comics. There's no one anywhere close by to play with; no one to talk to. No internet. A party-line phone, so I can't even pick up the (rotary) phone and call my friends from school when I want to.

I might as well be living on another planet. A planet somewhere in the Final Frontier.

I turn on that big Zenith and clunk the dial forward, past the lower stations, all the way up to Channel 42—the channel with the absolute worst reception of the four we can pick up with our antenna.

Living as we do nearly fifty miles from the nearest television station, I have my choice of three clear TV channels along with that one very weak and distorted one. The ABC, NBC, and PBS channels come in quite strong. Unfortunately, I'm only interested in the fare broadcast by the UHF station. Because while the others present a much better picture quality, Channel 42 from Birmingham, Alabama, offers a show this eight-year-old is experiencing for the very first time: *Star Trek*.

And what a life-changing show it is.

And now a quick verb-tense shift as I confirm that, yes, the Guardian was right: When I as an eight-year-old watched *Star Trek*, I experienced the greatest special effects I'd ever seen, before or since. For me, they were the best special effects in the history of television.

Not that I could actually *see* them.

Allow me to explain.

There are two varieties of "over-the-air" television broadcasts: VHF (Very High Frequency) and UHF (Ultra High Frequency). VHF occupies the lower numbers, from channels 2-13, and the signals on those frequencies tend to travel a greater distance and to provide a clearer picture. The UHF channels are more "line-of-sight," meaning there needs to be an unbroken line between the transmission antenna and the reception antenna on your set. Consequently, UHF signals tend to be weaker, the pictures distorted and filled with "snow," unless you live very close to the station or have a very tall antenna. (My dad, who lived down the road from us, stuck his UHF antenna atop his hundred-foot-tall HAM Radio tower, giving him a crystal-clear picture on the UHF channels—something I was insanely jealous of!)

If a show I wanted to watch came on ABC or NBC (or, very rarely, PBS), I was thrilled, because I could just relax and soak it in. But if it came on CBS—or, in the case of *Star Trek*, was syndicated as reruns that had been purchased by the local CBS station, to be shown at odd times such as the middle of a weekday afternoon—I had to watch it via that danged UHF channel.

And that meant I had work to do. I couldn't just sit back and passively absorb it. I had to help it out a bit. Or at least my *imagination* did.

So, no, the actual visual effects on *Star Trek*, I have to admit now, looking back at it with objectivity, were perhaps not quite as good as I was thinking they were.

But, back then, I was *sure* they were good. In fact, they were great. I could *tell*. I could *sense* it. I just *knew* it!

I couldn't actually *see* the effects, of course. Not very well. They were always obscured by a cloud of electronic snow. Our antenna wasn't high enough, and we lived too far away from Birmingham.

But, in my *head*? In my *imagination*?

In my mind, the *Enterprise* soared across beautifully-rendered starscapes and orbited above planets whose surfaces appeared utterly realistic. The Starfleet uniforms were not cheap velour but top-of-the-line material. The bridge of the *Enterprise* came straight from some future documentary on actual starship designs. And the alien worlds looked utterly real and awe-inspiring and occasionally terrifying.

I now know, of course, that the costumes and effects were done on a shoestring. Watching the show today, I'm always struck by how *different* it looks from how it came across to me the first time. From how I *imagined* it. It's like it's not even the same show.

But to the snow-filled and wonder-struck eyes of an eight-year-old in 1976?

Man, those effects were *spectacular*.

Because they played out not just before my eyes but inside my head. And the brain is the greatest special effects studio that has ever existed.

My imagination carried me across the galaxy along with Captain Kirk and Mr. Spock and Dr. McCoy and the rest.

And what an amazing—and highly *impactful*—voyage it was, for this little kid in the mid-Seventies.

Part of my brain was watching and imagining these dazzling visuals, yes. Another part of my mind, however, was absorbing, learning, growing, and being enlightened by what I was experiencing.

Star Trek truly was a voice in the wilderness for me.

It entertained me, yes. But it also educated me. It *inspired* me. It made me a *better person* than I likely otherwise would have become. I doubt this not a bit.

There in the depths of the Cold War, at a time filled with pessimism and the lingering psychological effects of the Vietnam War and the Watergate scandal, those syndicated *Star Trek* reruns provided us all a vision of hope. At a time of "We interrupt this program for a special report"—oh, no, are the nukes flying?!—*Star Trek* showed us a future filled with optimism and promise. A future where Mankind not only survived but *thrived*, becoming a force for good in a "Wild West" (Final) Frontier galaxy of Klingons and Romulans and Gorn and Tholians and all the rest. It showed me a future where the men and women of today (and was there ever a more "today" guy than James T. Kirk?) could go toe-to-toe with aliens and monsters and occasionally even half-mad space gods, and always prevail. And those "today" men and women would prevail not just because of their amazing future-technology (which often wasn't even as advanced as that of their adversaries) or because of their future-educated (or Vulcan!) brains, but because of their *basic human decency*.

Star Trek looked futuristic, but it felt current. It dealt with race relations and ethical dilemmas and present-day hot-button issues. And it did it all as a sort of metaphor or analogy for the times in which it first aired. It gave us John F Kennedy—I mean James T. Kirk—and the USS *Enterprise* American aircraft carrier—I mean Federation heavy cruiser, but hey, it had "USS" right there in the name!—exploring Kennedy's New Frontier—I mean Roddenberry's *Final* Frontier…! It's not too terrible of an exaggeration to say that Kirk could on occasion solve a planet's problems through a dramatic reading of the U.S. Constitution—the document, not the ship!

Star Trek taught ethics. It taught right from wrong. It taught respect for all life, and all life forms, and for the diversity of living things.

Understand: Diversity was *not* something I was seeing much of, living in rural Alabama. So, getting to see Lieutenants Sulu and Uhura, for example—utterly cool, competent, professional, and fun characters who also just happened to be of Japanese and African ethnicity—was incredibly beneficial for me. It allowed me as an eight-year-old to understand that human beings of any ethnicity could achieve great things. That people from all sorts of different backgrounds could work together on that bridge, as a cohesive whole, and their race and national origin meant literally nothing. How else but through television was I going to truly be able to learn that, in rural 1976 Alabama?

Star Trek has been rightly hailed as a pioneer in featuring a diverse cast in command positions on television, and I for one can testify that it did have a strong impact on at least one young and impressionable mind.

I have no idea which episode of *Star Trek* was the first one I ever saw; which of them was the first to smack me in the face with a moral or ethical lesson wrapped in a package of sweet entertainment. It very likely might have been "The Menagerie," because I have vivid memories of how much I was scared by the two aliens with giant, veiny heads who lived in the cave. Thinking back on it now, it's kind of a miracle I gave the show a chance and continued after that. Why did I? Probably because of the ending of that particular story. It was deeper and far more profound than I'd been led to expect by the action-related (and mild horror-related) events leading up to it.

Clearly this show had something to say. Now, I won't tell you that I, as an eight-year-old, consciously thought, "Hey, this show has a powerful moral message, so I'm going to tune in again tomorrow!" Nothing of the sort. But I will tell you that, even as a little kid, I could *sense* it. I could feel that there were bigger things going on here than just beating the Klingons and blowing up the monsters and firing the laser (*phaser!*) guns and whatnot.

"The Doomsday Machine" enthralled me with nearly an hour of

all-out action—not just one but two Federation starships struggling to stop a massive, world-destroying berserker vessel—followed by a conclusion that stressed the ideas of sacrifice and redemption. Over and over, this series would pull me in with its action and adventure, and then, once my shields were lowered, hit me right between the eyes with a moral lesson.

A little while later I saw "The Devil in the Dark," and that one scared me to death all over again. And again, by the time we got to the ending, I learned that there was more going on than it had first seemed. Yes, there was a monster, but that monster was just a mom protecting her kids. Respect—and make a deal with—the horrifying creature? Co-exist with it? Mind-blowing (and mind-expanding) stuff for a little kid living out in the woods.

"Mirror, Mirror," with its alternate-universe evil empire and its nasty-behaving crew, reinforced the idea of just how good and just and decent "our own" Enterprise crew truly was—because just look how different they could be, if they let all the power at their disposal corrupt them! In more recent times that episode has all but launched its own franchise of alternate-universe episodes of every other Trek series that has come along, and it's become a cliche to have the evil version of a TV character wear Spock's "evil goatee." But beyond those superficialities, there's still that central message: Power corrupts, and you have to be very, very careful not to allow it to change you for the worse. Kansas's Superman exhibits that trait, and so does Iowa's Kirk.

So profound an impact did even the trappings of *Star Trek* have on me, I found myself wondering why the Skipper on *Gilligan's Island* wore a blue Science uniform instead of a gold Command shirt. (Clearly Gilligan worked in Security because there was no way he was from Engineering!)

One last verb-tense shift here as I reach up, turn off that big Zenith color TV, and step back through the invisible portal. (It's the portal from "The City on the Edge of Forever," yes. That Harlan Ellison masterpiece is one that scarcely needs mentioning, because surely at this point everyone knows how incredible and important it is. Kirk falls in love with a radiant young Joan Collins and then has to prevent Dr. McCoy from saving her because, if he does so, history will be forever altered–and for the infinitely worse! So much to think about there.)

So here I am, back on the world of the Guardian of Forever. Alabama was pretty much as I remembered it, for better and for worse. How I survived those years in the wilderness is still a mystery, but a large part of the answer is found in my being able to watch TV shows like *Star Trek*. They taught me so much, yes–and they also saved me from such despair and loneliness.

"Time has resumed its shape. All is as it was before."

"Hey, I'm back. Thank you very much for that trip, Mr. Guardian of Forever. Though, honestly, I don't always love going back to my old hometown *now*. I probably could've done without revisiting it *back then*."

"Many such journeys are possible. Let me be your gateway."

"Yeah, uh, no thanks. I think I'm good, for now."

"...Perhaps someday in the future...?"

"Plexico to *Enterprise*. Come in, *Enterprise*."

"...Because it does get awfully boring down here, even for one such as I, and..."

"Scott here."

"...Did I mention it's been since before your sun burned hot in space..."

"One to beam up, Mr. Scott."

"...that anyone has asked me a question and—"

I wonder if the Guardian can pick up UHF transmissions?

"Energize!"

Van Allen Plexico writes novels, stories, and nonfiction books about nearly everything. A member of the Science Fiction and Fantasy Writers of America (SFWA), he is the author of twenty novels, a quarter of which have won a "Best Novel" award for that year. He cites the original *Star Trek* as a major influence on his life and work, and he looks forward to the day when Jim decides to do a book like this about *Space: 1999*.

THE DEREK IN THE DARK

BY DEREK TYLER ATTICO

Let me tell you a *Star Trek* story.

It's 1973, and I'm six years old. In the larger world around me Richard M. Nixon is the President of the United States. There's something bad going on in the world, it's called the Vietnam War.

Elvis performed in Hawaii, and the World Trade Center opened. For a kid my age, I had a pretty good understanding of these things. I remember not understanding the point of a war, watching clips of Elvis performing in Hawaii, and asking my parents to take me to the Twin Towers. I wanted to go to the top of the tallest buildings on earth.

My own world may not have been as vast, but it was just as important. I was in the first grade, and I was already reading Shakespeare. The Bard's tales had become part of my Bedtime stories that, by this time, I was reading on my own. When I was two or three, my mom started me on Dr. Seuss and pop-up books and then quickly graduated me to Grimms Fairy tales, Edgar Allan Poe, Greek Mythology, and Alexandre Dumas. Reading took my young mind to places and time periods that could only be visited through the power of imagination.

I lived in the Bronx, but I went to school in Harlem. On the weekdays, I'd stay with my grandmother, who lived only a few blocks from the public school I attended. However, on the weekends, my parents would pick me up, and I'd return to my home in the Bronx.

For a six-year-old, this was the best of both worlds.

I had two sets of friends, two homes, two cooking styles (Grandma's was the best!), two neighborhoods, and two types of adult supervision. During the week, my grandmother's rules and schedule were simple: She was my grandmother, and I was the kid. As long as I listened to her rules and followed her schedule, there was lots of room for fun. Sometimes we'd have tea parties together. On most days, I'd watch the old *Batman* TV show at 4:30 pm, and on the days I didn't watch TV, there was enough time to play with my friends. Whatever I did, dinner was at six, and I had to be in bed by 8 pm. This, of course, was non-negotiable with my grandmother. On occasions when I tried to break that contract, she'd give me a look or say a few words that would have me fall back in line quickly.

The 8 pm bedtime was torture because every kid knew all the best stuff, (the TV shows for adults) came on at night. On Fridays, The *Six Million Dollar Man* aired on ABC at 8 pm, a fact that made me cry myself to sleep on more than one occasion to my grandmother's disregard.

The weekends, however, were much different.

Like myself, my parents used the weekends to unwind and get away from rules and schedules. We'd often sleep in late, getting up to have pancakes for lunch and going out to the movies to catch an 8 pm show or later!

When we stayed at home, sometimes my mom would let me stay up past midnight watching old movies.

There was always a television on in our home in the Bronx, and usually, it was more than one. This was because my father built them. Back then, when a television broke down, you didn't just buy a new one—that was far too expensive—you had your TV repaired. Someone would make a house call, actually, come to your home and fix your broken television. If you lived anywhere in the five boroughs back then, it was a good chance the person coming to your home was my dad.

My father was a regional television repairman for Zenith Electronics. So, the televisions in our home weren't items that had been purchased in a store but one-of-a-kind "contraptions" that he had created. Our living room TV looked more like a floor model in a department store. A twenty-eight-inch screen with sliding doors to reveal a radio, record player, and vinyl records, with a remote control!

Our dining room table also doubled as my father's workshop table, where he'd build and repair televisions. One Saturday, he was working on a medium-sized tabletop television while it was on, something he often did. The pretty faux wood cover for the TV had been removed, and the skeletal innards of the device were exposed. Glass tubes of various sizes sprouted out of the back of the television set like some alien vegetable with budding tubes. Directly or indirectly, all the tubes fed into one massive central housing that held the largest tube in the television—called the picture tube. It was called this because while the back of it was just another tube my father was used to repairing, its front was a screen the entire world watched.

Unlike the world, I was usually more interested in watching my father work. What went on inside a television, how it worked, how it was put together was usually more interesting than the programs that played on it. Except for *Batman* and *The Six Million Dollar Man*, reading, not television, was my thing.

But this Saturday was different.

On the screen, there was a man in a blue shirt with pointed ears. I had been watching him talk to another man in a gold shirt—his captain, about a monster that was terrorizing some space town. The creature had killed people, and now they were going to catch and kill it. The monster was large and scary to my young eyes. It appeared to be some kind of living pulsating rock that could burn men alive. These two men had guns that seemed to be very powerful, and they were confident they could kill the creature if necessary.

But they wanted to try another way.

The captain's name was Kirk, and the strange man in the blue shirt was called Spock. Spock said he could talk to the living rock and see into its mind. When he touched it, he was in great pain because the creature was, his voice was full of it. I could feel it, he started crying, and when he spoke, I understood it wasn't really him but the creature's voice speaking through him. As they spoke together, I learned the rock wasn't a monster at all, it was a mother trying to protect her children! Kirk and Spock understood this, and so did I! I loved my mom and knew that she protected me every day. I realized Kirk and Spock must've been thinking about their moms, too, because I could feel the episode shift. They weren't talking about killing anymore but saving the creature, saving everyone, and finding a way for everyone on the planet to live together. They called a doctor named McCoy, and he healed the alien. They had found another way.

My father leaned over from the back of the television set, I'd forgotten he was there. I was so immersed that I felt like I was in the cavern with Kirk, Spock, McCoy, and the alien creature. I'd lost all track of everything except what was happening in the world on that color screen. He could see it in my eyes, the wonder and the excitement.

"That's *Star Trek*," my father told me.

The rest of the weekend was a blur. I couldn't stop thinking about these two guys that hadn't done what everyone always does on TV or in the world—they didn't kill the creature. They talked to it. Even at that age, I understood there was violence in the world, even if I didn't understand the full scope of that violence. I knew there were wars going on and that everyone agreed wars were bad, but for some reason, people died anyway. My parents taught me that there was violence in the world, but the use of violence should never be the first action but the absolute last. "It's always better to talk to people than to fight them," they'd always tell me. And now I was seeing Kirk and Spock do just what I had been told was the best thing to do.

After the weekend at school, I tried to tell my friends what I'd seen, but all the kids were talking about the latest episode of *The Six Million Dollar Man*, something my grandmother had made sure I knew nothing about. One of my friends humored me and let me tell him about what I'd seen. Before I was halfway through, he interrupted me, "I've seen that one. It was kinda boring. Watch the one with the ship. The ship is cool," he said. What my friend said made no sense to me. Nothing I'd seen was boring, and I couldn't wait to watch the next episode.

During that next week, I didn't leave anything to chance. I checked *TV Guide* (for those that don't know, this wasn't an option on the television in those days. It was a small, condensed weekly book that told you everything that was on the only five or six channels everyone watched. You could pick them up at a newsstand, but both my parents and grandmother had a subscription.) and confirmed that *Star Trek* would indeed be on again Saturday at 6 pm on Channel 11 WPIX.

The episode was called "The Corbomite Maneuver," whatever that meant.

This time I wasn't looking at whatever TV my father had sitting on the dining room table as he worked on it. I was lying on the floor in front of our TV in the living room at 6 pm, and I could see that my friend was wrong.

The ship wasn't just cool, it was beautiful. Even as a kid, it was clear to me that there was something elegant and powerful yet simple in the design of the ship. A disc with three tubes. The disc was where the people worked, Two of the tubes were obviously the engines, and the third had to be where they all lived when not working. The windows unconsciously translated the scale of the vessel to my young mind. I realized it was massive. With humanity's recent manned trips to the moon (the last was Apollo 17 in 1972), it was clear that this ship was larger than anything humans would have for a long time.

Her name was *Enterprise*, and I was in love.

As I watched my friends Kirk and Spock from last week exploring the galaxy in their mighty vessel, I experienced the unexpected. They came upon a cube that wouldn't get out of their way, so they had to destroy it because it was harmful. The alien that built the cube came looking for it in a giant glowing sphere that the *Enterprise* crew said was over a mile in diameter. As a kid, that was hard to imagine. A mile was a distance I was used to for measuring land masses and for traveling somewhere far away. At the beginning of the episode, the *Enterprise* was the largest ship I could imagine, and now there was another ship, something the size of a city, looming over it. The immense alien ship somehow held the *Enterprise* in its grip, and everything I watched Kirk and Spock do to try and get free failed.

This time the alien didn't like them at all. He called them primitive savages, and I remember thinking, unlike the previous week, for this guy, now Kirk, Spock, and the *Enterprise* were the monsters, and the alien didn't seem interested in talking. I watched the adults lose patience with each other on the ship, mainly because some of them were scared. I'd seen this from time to time on TV and with adults I knew. But I also saw something else, something I was very familiar with. The crew was disciplined, and even though they were afraid, that discipline kept them from falling apart. Even as a kid, I understood that. My grandmother's discipline kept me calm, especially when I wasn't on schedule. She always told me to "follow through, finish what you start, no matter what." To me, it looked like even though Kirk, Spock, and the Enterprise seemed outmatched, they didn't quit.

Kirk was looking for a way to follow through and not give up.

When Kirk couldn't find a way using the rules, he made one up. I didn't know anything about poker or bluffing, but I understood Kirk told the alien a story. A story he hoped he would believe. When the alien bought the story Kirk told him, it gave Kirk the one thing he desired more of: time. That time gave the captain what he needed, an opportunity to save his crew and his ship. And when the tables did turn, and the *Enterprise* crew disabled the alien vessel, Kirk still came to his rescue.

Star Trek taught me a valuable lesson that day.

I saw that there was no problem that couldn't be solved through thought and determination. In both episodes, Kirk and Spock had the opportunity to use violence and aggression, but instead of a fist, they used quick thinking and compassion to resolve conflicts. That's how my parents were raising me, and that's what *Star Trek* was telling me the future could and would be if enough of us worked together.

After those two episodes, I watched *Star Trek* every Saturday without fail for years. Sure, there were episodes where phasers and photon torpedoes were used first, and questions asked later. But even then, these were done to show the folly, and the futility of war and senseless violence.

My parents set out to give me a strong sense of decency, morality, and character that would allow me to navigate the world and contribute to it. A mind that wouldn't fear science but would embrace it, utilize it, and love it. A sense of understanding that could see people and events openly and truthfully.

I find myself fortunate to have watched *Star Trek* during my formative years. Would I be the same person I am today without *Star Trek*?

The honest answer is no.

Star Trek has had an impact on me throughout my life. As a kid, it helped to reinforce in a cool and exciting way the values and ideals my parents were working to instill within me. When my friends would playfight like Kirk, I'd use logic to make my argument about something or give my version of a "Kirk speech" to think my way out of something or convince them about an argument I was making. Most of the time, this just infuriated my friends, which always delighted me.

As an adult, *Star Trek* gave me my first professional sale as a writer and set me on a path I'm thankful for. I truly believe this is because, in all the important ways, I've never lost that awe and wonder I had as a six-year-old watching Kirk and Spock in a darkened cave with a monster but seeing something else entirely.

Derek Tyler Attico is a science fiction author, essayist, and photographer. He won the Excellence in Playwriting Award from the Dramatist Guild of America. Derek is also a two-time winner of the Star Trek Strange New Worlds short story contest ("Alpha & Omega," "The Dreamer and the Dream") published by Simon and Schuster. Derek is also the author of the upcoming *The Autobiography of Benjamin Sisko* from Titan Books.

MY SUNDAY MORNINGS AT 10:00 AM

BY GORDON DYMOWSKI

To say that *Star Trek* has influenced me would be an understatement. I think it would be more appropriate to say that it has impacted my life since I was born.

Seriously. I was born two days before the episode "The Ultimate Computer" was broadcast. You know, the one in which a pre-Blacula/King of Cartoons William Marshall invents a new supercomputer that runs the *Enterprise* and destroys several ships in the process? The one where Kirk was referred to as Captain "Dunsel" because he was being made useless? (Spoiler: things got better after that episode)

According to family legend (mostly via my mother), I first saw *Star Trek* as a one-year-old, sitting in a highchair while my dad was taking care of me. Since Mom was out, Dad was feeding me potato chips because he wanted to be the "cool" dad. Since I hadn't learned how to eat anything, much less potato chips, I scratched myself and began crying. Although I have no memory of what transpired when Mom returned, I can only imagine that it consisted of strong words, scolding, and parental reassurance.

(I have no idea which episode I was watching, or even whether this was during the initial run of the series. However, fun fact: the final, original episode of the Original Series was "Turnabout Intruder" which was shown in June 1969, and I will always associate that episode with minor childhood trauma regardless of the truth)

But my "official" introduction to classic *Star Trek* came in 1975, as it was shown on Sunday mornings at 10 am on WGN Channel 9 at the time. At the time, I was about eight years old and serving as a substitute altar boy for my local parish. That's right—a "substitute" altar boy, meaning that when someone couldn't serve the 6 am Mass (or had problems following the 7:30 am Polish Sunday Mass), I was the guy they called.

But Sunday mornings on Chicago television were a wonderland of interesting, offbeat programming. If I could catch it early enough, I might see *The New Zoo Review*. Maybe I might luck out and see *Mario and the Magic Movie Machine* (which did great, imaginative things with stock footage) or *Marshall Efron's Simplified and Painless Sunday School* (which was much better than going to church). But at 8:30 am, there was *Gigglesnort Hotel*, taking the characters I loved from my earlier childhood (such as the Dirty Dragon, Weird, and the Blog) and putting them in a near-sitcom situation.

I mention all of this because although they were quite humorous, they were a slightly odd lead-in to the two-hour block of programming that WGN held on Sunday mornings in my youth. I usually ate my breakfast around 9 am and then bathed and dressed. At ten o'clock, it was time for *Star Trek*, and if memory serves, my first episode proper was "A Taste of Armageddon." That was followed at eleven by *The Lone Ranger* and then *The Cisco Kid*. It was shown at a perfect time so that whether I attended/served 9 am or noon Mass, I could catch this strange show which took place in outer space. (Serving Noon Mass meant missing *The Cisco Kid*, but that was never one of my favorites. I avoided serving the ten-thirty am Sunday Mass because I had my priorities.)

But even at that young age, *Star Trek* seemed different than the science fiction I was used to watching. The first comic I ever bought was Superman tackling the Galactic Golem (you do the research for issue number and publication date, I have an essay to write.) My Saturday afternoons were spent watching *Svengoolie* on WFLD-TV, and you couldn't dial through the UHF channels without bumping into a show that was killing time with science fiction serials. (And I was part of that generation of Chicago fans who saw *Doctor Who* as a white-haired guy in a frilly shirt before he became the curly-haired guy with the scarf). But *Star Trek* was different...there was seriousness and intentionality to the show, even if I couldn't see it at the time. It felt more realistic than the other shows and books I was consuming. There was something simple in the tales about a starship that featured a straightforward leader, his slightly brainy friend, the other curmudgeonly friend, and…

Well, I lived in a middle-class neighborhood in Chicago. After school, I would hang out with my best friend Bobby and his family. Part of the reason was that I was an only child, my cousins were all spread out, and my mother worked full-time. Yes, I had the classic everyone-knew-each-other-on-our-street upbringing that fosters eye-rolling from the younger generation. My parents were divorced, which made things difficult in my Catholic parish. Besides, my father and I did not get along except for two things we shared besides genetics: a love of Sherlock Holmes and classic *Star Trek*.

We would watch it together and for one hour, there was peace when we were together. But one of the great things about *Star Trek* (without the later "The Original Series" subtitle) was that it was a gateway into imagination, Sure, I had Planet of the Apes action figures (and was present for the whole "Gorilla My Dreams" week series of movies at 3:30 pm on Channel 7), but there was something about *Star Trek* that felt more imaginative, more participatory, more *hopeful*. (One of my happier memories was heading downtown with Dad to the Chicago Theater to catch *Star Trek: The Motion Picture* on opening day. And don't get me started on how I would marathon *Star Trek: The Wrath of Khan* at the Brighton Theater on Dollar Tuesday night the same way my mother would marathon *A Hard Day's Night* when she was my age…but I digress).

One Christmas was especially memorable as I had acquired several long-desired items: action figures of Kirk and Spock, but also the infamous Mego Enterprise playset. I say "infamous" not because it was malevolent or nasty, but because it had a "working" transporter. Simply place your action figure in the transporter, spin the blue knob, press the green button, and it disappears, transported to… somewhere. Sure, the play set also included an actual captain's chair, console, and two stools, but that transporter was the awesome and intriguing centerpiece. (Especially when I realized that the "transporter" was simply a plastic cylinder with two empty alcoves on either side. Place my Kirk action figure in one cubicle, transport him away, and place Cornelius from Planet of the Apes in the other, and instant transporter malfunction! Well, that's how my brain worked back then, and I refuse to apologize for it.)

But back to *Star Trek* and Dad...since my father was an attorney, I wasn't so much scolded or berated when I misbehaved as much as I was cross-examined. My dad was a lawyer, and sometimes I felt like I was stuck in the last ten minutes of *Perry Mason* when Raymond Burr would cross-examine the guilty party. (If you need a more contemporary example, think of the last ten minutes of *Law & Order* with Sam Waterston as Jack McCoy). My father was also a typical 1950s-era man raised by first-generation immigrants: my grandmother was from Lithuania, and my grandfather was from Poland. In his opinion, men didn't have or express feelings; only women did so, and my mother was making me less of a man by encouraging it.

Misogyny, thy name is Richard. And yes, I would provoke him by calling him "Dick," why do you ask?

So, it's no wonder that the first Trek character with whom I identify was Spock—after all, he was in the same boat I was. Emotionally unavailable father with unreasonable expectations, an emotional mother who tried her best to deal with a very dysfunctional family relationship...the script just writes itself, and its name is "Journey to Babel." There's no better metaphor for a Gen X male who is raised by Boomer parents, especially if that male's father is raised by second-generation immigrants and enjoys nothing but Westerns, war movies, and gangster films. Navigating Dad's limited emotional range (from anger to resentment) could be tricky, and Spock managed it as well as he could. Sure, he had emotional outbursts, but usually due to external circumstances like alien spores, *pon farr*, or the charms of Mariette Hartley.

But when he needed to be cold and logical, Spock was my go-to reference. After all, this was a man who was willing to let Kirk's love die for history to move correctly. Sacrificing an officer or two on a shuttle mission. Determining that the Horta wasn't acting out of malice, but out of maternal concern for her children. It was a good lesson to learn as a child: sometimes you need to control your emotions, and other times you need to let loose and simply *feel*. Despite getting criticized by his father early on, and later Doctor McCoy, well...

One digression and I promise I'll resume the nostalgia: Does anyone *else* feel that McCoy's insults weren't just good-natured joshing? For someone trained in medicine, specializing in non-human life forms, McCoy is very pointed in his criticism of Spock. "Pointy-eared" and "green-blooded" may be "facts," but they always came off as a bit harsh. Given my issues with parental criticism, this may just be an overgeneralization on my part. However, as much as McCoy might have been the "voice of reason" between Kirk and Spock, I think the writers of the classic series overplayed their hand. Especially since I wish they would have introduced Chekhov's phaser, or the writing principle which states that when you introduce a phaser in Act One, you use it to shoot Ensign Chekhov in the third act.

What I'm trying to say is that I found Ensign Chekhov annoying as a kid. End of digression.

The other major character I resonated with as a kid was Lieutenant Montgomery Scott, aka "Scotty," Chief Engineer of the *USS Enterprise*. Granted, I had neither the desire nor mathematical ability to become an engineer, yet Scotty's primary personality traits seemed to fit me well. His ability to solve problems on the fly, taking what might be possible and defying the odds, was something that I aspired toward when I was a child. Between Scotty's problem-solving ability and Spock's logical analyses, I learned how to manage myself in any problematic work or school situation. It never came easy, and only solidified after many years of practice and therapy, but I learned that I was more resourceful than I realized when it came to difficult situations.

But Scotty also taught me another important lesson—the importance of having fun. This was a man whose idea of dealing with alien invaders forcing the *Enterprise* to fly towards another galaxy was to get them drunk. Although he would end up falsely accused of a crime, Scotty was the first to head down to a planet to enjoy revelry. Montgomery Scott managed to be both a "miracle worker" and the kind of man who wrote technical manuals in his *spare time*. Sure, Scotty loved engineering but also knew when to, as the kids say, "Party down in party town." It was a trait that I carried into adulthood, and that I also try to practice in my current life, much to the chagrin of my many editors.

But if I'm completely honest (and I have no reason not to be), the main way in which *Star Trek* impacted me was that it inspired me to become a writer.

One of my more endearing traits (at least, I find it endearing) is a curiosity about the names onscreen. Sure, I could tell the difference between William Shatner and Leonard Nimoy, but every *Star Trek* episode asked a question that I needed to have answered:

Who the heck was Gene Roddenberry?

After all, I was young enough to figure out that the host of *Night Gallery* had also hosted *The Twilight Zone*...and wrote many of the episodes as well. Several shows I watched as a child were "A Quinn Martin Production," as if he was someone I should know. Scripts featuring that Columbo guy were written by a pair of men known as "Richard Levinson and William Link." As a child, I wanted to learn more about the people behind the names, especially the ones that followed the "Written by" credit. Gene Roddenberry, whose name came at the very front of the credits, was the ultimate mystery.

Learning about how Roddenberry "trained" himself as a writer—watching television to determine act structure, dialogue, and other aspects—helped me adopt a similar mode in writing my own stories. Watching classic *Star Trek* as a child, I realized one major fact about the show that enthralled me.

Star Trek was not just about social commentary but told stories that were morally complex and provided insights into values and culture.

Let's avoid talking about "Let That Be Your Last Battlefield," as it's the most didactic and obvious of classic Trek storytelling. (Plus, the only good thing about it was Frank Gorshin). As a child, I realized that this wasn't the ride-a-rocket-and-zap-the-bad-guys Flash Gordon serials that Ray Rayner showed in his program. *Star Trek* told tales where there wasn't a clear black-and-white issue, but tales that had a moral ambiguity in their plotting. Sure, classic *Star Trek* may have over-relied on the "this-planet-is-like-Earth-except-for-one-difference" trope, but it provided a context within which our heroes had to struggle.

Even the comedic episodes had something of a moral ambiguity to them. Thanks to a crashed spaceship and an abandoned book, a planet adopted a culture right out of *The Untouchables*. A con man finds a world of androids ready to serve him. Small, rapidly procreating fur balls threatened wheat supplies during a heated political conflict. All classic *Star Trek* tales impressed me as a child not because they were "about the social condition", but because they taught me three key facts about good storytelling.

Good storytelling is straightforward and clear and should not only *say* something but *mean* something.

As a child, *Star Trek* impressed upon me the idea that you could tell a story that had a deeper meaning that reflected the then-current social conditions. *Star Trek*'s tales were universal, often discussing "big issues" in a way that was clever and subtle unlike other late 1960s/early 1970s television shows which pursued "relevance." (I should know, growing up in the era of the After School Special and the "Very Special Episode.") Very rarely did the writers hit the viewer over the head with their messages (except in the third season, but that's another essay), and their themes came through the narrative. No long exposition or obvious "As You Know" moments, just letting the story tell itself and allowing the viewer to determine the message. It was more *Outer Limits* than *Twilight Zone* in its approach, but *Star Trek* managed to wear its heart and values on its sleeve without being obnoxious about it.

As I grew older, I began watching *Star Trek* (and other favorite shows) in a very Roddenberry-esque manner. I learned how to structure storytelling, how to use metaphor effectively, and making a greater point without hitting people over the head about it. (But yes, I would also watch shows simply for the fun of it). But I learned that any creative act hides its "art" and messaging in a good narrative, and that lesson is something I aspire toward in my work.

But as a kid, I loved how classic *Star Trek* engaged my imagination and curiosity. It's a love that has carried well into my adulthood, from Saturday nights in St. Louis after a *long* week of work to a radio conversation on the show's 50th anniversary with a then-fellow Chicago Nerd Social Club Board Member/now five-time Hugo Award-winning author[17].

But there will be nothing like the feeling of watching classic *Star Trek* on Sunday mornings, at ten am, on WGN Channel Nine.

Gordon Dymowski has been boldly going where no one has gone before since he was a young man. He has been a community organizer in St. Louis, a former counselor, and a member of several boards. Currently, he is a Chicago-based digital marketing consultant and copywriter by day and a New Pulp fiction writer by night. You can learn more about him via http://www.gordondymowski.com or http://bit.ly/GdymAuthor. Live long and prosper!

---

[17] Here's the receipt: https://www.wbez.org/stories/which-star-trek-is-your-trek/147a27d0-8018-41c9-bd31-7f355352499d

SUNSHINE AND SCI-FI

BY CORINNA BECHKO

I'm not from outer space, but in some ways I work there. I'm primarily a science fiction writer, occasionally a science fact writer, and almost always a writer of things that take place far from our cozy little cool-hued marble of a planet. Endless expanses, warped time, excruciatingly weird ways to die; all these live rent-free in my head. I might be making small talk about housing prices or traffic, but you can bet I'm instead thinking about how different the world would look if it possessed rings or a couple more moons.

All of which is to say I tend to obsess over the future rather than the past. Nostalgia isn't my natural state. That's why I was surprised by a rush of it when I saw a news item about a lavish nine-bedroom, thirteen-bath estate renting in Boca Raton, FL, for almost $200,000 a month. The listing boasted a waterfall pool, a wine cellar, and an overall "*Star Trek* theme." The unfamiliar feeling of wistful yearning wasn't the result of being born rich. My family was decidedly middle class, the three of us sharing a single bathroom my entire childhood. But the juxtaposition of *Star Trek* and Florida? That brought back a lot of memories.

To most people the Sunshine State seems exotic. Or at least weird. Maybe even dangerous. It's filled with stinging insects, biting reptiles, and wacky people willing to drop millions of dollars a year to live in a rental. But to me it's just home. It's the place I was born, the same as my mother and my grandfather before her. It's the place I went to school, learned to drive, and shared a first kiss. It's where my longest-lasting friendships were forged. And it's where I first learned you could work in space.

The specific town I'm from, Sarasota, is probably not at the top of most lists of futuristic cities. Where other towns had tech entrepreneurs, we had the winter quarters for the Ringling Brothers Circus.

I spent more time on beaches and in swamps than in gleaming glass buildings. When I was six, I came within inches of stepping on the head of an alligator twice my size. A couple of years later, camping with my Girl Scout troop, I learned how to call them. All of it left me with an abiding love of the natural world. And the knowledge that no matter how strange something seemed you could bet there was something even odder out there somewhere, waiting to be discovered.

Meanwhile, back at my house, things were decidedly more prosaic. In addition to sharing one bathroom my family also shared one air conditioner, an ancient wall unit that wheezed and rattled just above the lone TV on special occasions. The rest of the time we persevered, wilted and sweating, but in tune with the environment. I've often read accounts of kids rushing home from school to watch their favorite program. In Florida you don't rush anywhere if you don't have AC in your car or your home. Instead, I moseyed home, stood in front of the open refrigerator for far too long claiming I couldn't find anything to eat when I actually just wanted to feel the chill, then grabbed an orange (often fresh from the backyard tree) and a piece of cheese before decamping to the living room.

Fortunately, my mother recognized that no homework was going to get done during the worst heat of the day. On the rare occasions she insisted I dramatically demonstrated counterarguments: the humidity rendered the Xeroxed worksheets too moist for sums, my sharpened pencil tearing through the saturated paper. The sultry air made me drowsy, my head dropping lower and lower until a damp half-moon formed on the cover of my history book, courtesy of my forehead. The nuance of afternoon-penned essays was suspect, and please, don't even try to parse the spelling. Like people, thoughts move slowly when the ambient temperature tops 90 degrees F.

So, the afternoons became mine. Unlike a lot of Gen Xers, my mom only sometimes worked part-time outside the house. She was often home, busy with her own projects and concerns, but ready and willing to drive me to a friend's house or on an errand. Most of the time though, I turned on the television. After a couple of clicks of the attached dial the right channel was found, and I retreated to the couch beneath the open window to escape into an imaginary, hopefully cooler, world. It didn't occur to me that I was watching a syndicated block often showing series that had first aired before I was born. They were all new to me, until they weren't. But by the second time through I felt like, having discovered them, they belonged to me.

My mother never quite understood why I watched a lot of it. It was silly, she said, and not very dignified. She was not the type to ever censure my media consumption, but that didn't stop her from passing judgment. *Gilligan's Island* was her least favorite, possibly followed by *Battle of the Planets*. *The Twilight Zone* got a pass because it creeped her out and that earned it extra points by her reckoning. But original *Star Trek*? That one seemed to perplex her. I distinctly remember her walking into the room while I was watching the episode titled "The Enemy Within." Many people think that one should come with a content warning due to some very unethical behavior perpetrated by Captain Kirk, albeit enacted by his twisted dark side. What set my mother off was something else entirely: a small dog wearing a unicorn horn and antennae, barking madly.

"Is that dog," she attempted to say while laughing almost too hard to get the words out, "wearing a unicorn horn? With *antennae*?"

"It's an alien," I muttered defensively, stung that she wasn't taking this very serious show more seriously.

"Uh huh," she said, wandering off as soon as the scene shifted. "Homework right after dinner, okay?"

My dad was a different story. On the rare occasions he made it home early we would pack up dinner and head to the beach. It was cooler there, incredibly lovely, and, at least during the summer, nearly empty of people. Since we lived on the Gulf Coast there would often be an astounding sunset as we pulled chilled fruit salad and cheese sandwiches out of our worn cooler. My father worked outside all day doing phone line repair so he couldn't face hot dinners during the summer. That suited my mom since the last thing she wanted to do was heat the house further with the oven. Sharing a meal as flocks of seabirds crossed the setting sun on their way to their offshore roosts felt like coming back to life. Gradually my brain began to form coherent thoughts as my body cooled. The power of speech returned. And as often as not, we would discuss whatever I was currently reading or watching. My mom might find some of it ridiculous, but my dad had a much higher tolerance for all things science fiction. If *The Lord of the Rings* was on my mind Mom would weigh in. But time travel and alternate dimensions were strictly my father's purview.

When I think back on it now those beachside dinners seem almost otherworldly themselves. Sand as white as sugar, air thick enough to feel, and a line of dolphins cavorting just past the breakers as they caught their own dinners. I've lived in California for decades at this point, near deserts filled with sagebrush and beaches the color of dirt which don't seem as foreign to me now as they once did. But those long-ago picnics under the emerging stars, Venus bright on the horizon, still shine in my dreams. It all seemed quite ordinary then, the only wonders being those that were conjured during discussions with my father.

Big ideas were bandied about, fueled by the media I'd consumed earlier that afternoon. Things like the notion that all life on Earth, from the grapes we were sharing to those marine mammals and the fish they chased out in the Gulf to my parents and I, proved to be carbon-based. I would have never thought to ask about this basic fact if it wasn't for "The Devil in the Dark," one of my favorite episodes of all time. Could there really be silicon-based life out there somewhere?

My father didn't know off-hand, having never traveled beyond the Earth himself, but he had a hunch. It was possible, but not probable. Carbon creates more complex bonds with other elements than silicon can, giving rise to more possibilities. Dad didn't stop there, though. He made sure that we watched *Cosmos* together later, allowing Carl Sagan to explain these things in terms even a fourth grader from Florida could understand.

The lessons stuck, going far beyond the rudiments of the periodic table. The more you learned the more you could imagine, apparently. A grounding in science didn't unweave the rainbow. Instead, it sparked curiosity. Maybe there were parts of the rainbow you couldn't know through vision alone? And just like that, the world became a little more interesting, and a lot more beautiful.

Still, I had other kinds of questions. In a universe filled with so much strangeness, were there any constants? Would a sentient rock, for instance, really feel love for its kids?

My mother did have an opinion this time.

"Yup," she said, completely convinced. "It just makes sense that other creatures would feel love. For their children, for their friends, for their pets too. How could they not?" She had often told me it was important to treat my various animals well because they loved me. To do otherwise would be a betrayal.

So, love is logical. That felt right, even if Mr. Spock might not quite sign on to this interpretation. Extending the idea beyond the immediate family and even species did too. Perhaps my favorite afternoon siesta show was serious after all, despite what anyone else thought.

That idea, that something could be serious as well as fun, was always important to me. I was an only child, a weirdo who liked hanging around with adults if they were willing to talk to me about dinosaurs, music, and science fiction. I was lucky enough to have lots of these in my life. But as adventurous as many of them were in a variety of ways, very few of them qualified as scientists. Yet that's what I yearned towards when I let myself think through what I'd like to be when I grew up. It wasn't exactly a popular choice for girls growing up in small towns in the South.

But if there's one thing that comes up a lot in *Trek* it's that everyone is from somewhere, and often that place is far from the center of the galaxy. Even Kirk is from a small town on Earth. The women of the Enterprise were often from places even more remote, at least to a kid like me. And yet, through hard work and talent, they got their dream postings. It didn't seem impossible that I might too. Now if I could just figure out what that might mean. In practice most science seemed a lot like math, at least at school. My mom hated math, even though she was interested in a lot of the more people-focused fields, like anthropology and archeology. My dad liked math and could have gone to MIT if he had made different choices himself. But like any good TOS episode, life is all about moral quandaries. The difference, of course, is that they are seldom wrapped up in under an hour.

The crew of the *Enterprise* often solved their problems with science, even if that science was, upon closer inspection, a lot of hand-waving combined with some science-adjacent words. But they never solved things *just* with science. Even Spock, Mr. Logic himself, took it as gospel that the humane answer was the truest. Sometimes that led to rather extreme solutions (must Edith Keeler really die?) but I never doubted that he was thinking of the greater good. Selfishness was for literal dirtbags with names like Mudd.

All of which implied that science, being a human endeavor, necessitated a human component even when the problem could be solved with pure physics. So, what if I wasn't a math whiz? Instead, I was someone who could conjure sympathy for any creature, be they Horta, Mugato, or Alpha 177 canine. My favorite space farers were like me in that respect, and they wore it proudly. It was a strength, not a weakness. Perhaps a career in space wasn't out of the question after all.

It's odd to look back on all of it now, from a vantage point that includes a science degree (in zoology, to no one's surprise) and several decades working for nonprofits where the moral quandaries are massive, constant, and immediate. I don't know if I've gone a week in that entire time without being reminded of the "The Devil in the Dark" and the happy collaboration between the unexpected lifeform and the miners on Janus VI once they finally understood each other. It's rare for such a thing to occur in the real world, but not unheard of. But even if the episode is far from realistic, I think it's something better. It's aspirational, pointing at a marriage between empathy and science that couldn't have happened if either were in short supply.

With apologies to my mother and father who certainly shaped the person I became, it isn't a stretch to say that encountering TOS when I did pushed me towards ideas and onto paths I might not otherwise have explored. My own writing tends to blend politics and science fiction. I like to place people in extreme situations, far from home, then hit them with an intractable problem. It's never made me "mansion money," but then again, would I want that? It's hard not to lust after a *Star Trek*-themed screening room, waterfront views, and enough cash to host all my friends for a massive pool party.

Upon further reflection, I'm almost certain Spock would tell me that the idea of this mansion must die. It was obviously built on a pristine beach like the ones I cherished as a child. It's ostentatious, wasteful, and sits heavily on the land it occupies. Many creatures, perhaps not sentient but certainly possessing feelings, lost their homes when it was built.

So, instead, I will remind myself that luxury was never a component of my childhood. My recollections are untouched by anything that happened to my home state after I left. Now that I live in the land of the Gorn, close to the spot where the iconic episode "Arena" was filmed, I'm arguably closer to the wellspring of my memories. But in my mind *Star Trek* will always taste a little like oranges and be lit by a tropical sun.

Corinna Bechko is a Hugo- and Eisner-nominated *New York Times* best-selling author who has worked for numerous publishers including DC, Marvel, Dark Horse, BOOM!, IDW and Sideshow on titles such as *Star Wars: Legacy, Savage Hulk, Invisible Republic, The Expanse, Avatar: Adapt or Die, Green Lantern: Earth One,* and several *Star Trek* short stories. Her books for young readers include *Smithsonian Dig it: Dinosaurs* and *Smithsonian 1001 Super Space Facts*. She spends her days at the Natural History Museum of Los Angeles County where she works as a fossil preparator.

SATURDAYS AND STARSHIPS

BY AARON SMITH

Monday through Friday, at six in the evening, Dan Rather would come on at dinnertime and tell us about the world we lived in. But on Saturdays, things were different, and it was James T. Kirk who led the tour through a universe that maybe could really be, someday, if we'd ever manage to get things right.

I was in early grammar school, and *Star Trek* was already more than fifteen years old, but it was new to me, and that's what mattered. By the time we started watching those Saturday evening reruns, I already liked science fiction and space fantasy. Of course I did, as a member of the first Star Wars generation. But this, well, this was different, a whole new era of human adventure unfolding before my eyes, chapter by chapter, week by week. It captured my imagination like nothing else had.

It was hopeful, it wasn't only about action and fighting, though it had plenty of that too. It was about more than that. It asked the question of, "What is humanity capable of if it ever gets its act together?" I didn't know it at the time, but that early exposure to *Star Trek* shaped my personality and moral compass far more than any school lesson or church sermon ever could.

But I wasn't thinking about such philosophical things then. I was just swept up in it all. The ships, the stars, the bright gold, blue, and red of the Starfleet uniforms, the strange aliens, the intrigue, the futuristic science, the suspense and joy and wonder of it all. I felt at home there, in this imaginary future.

I don't know what episode was my first, and I'm pretty sure I didn't see every one until much later, but there are moments and images I will hold in my heart for as long as I live. "Shore Leave" stands out. The vivid colors of the planet's surface, the moment when I really thought we'd lost Dr. McCoy, Kirk's fight with Finnegan.

And I don't think I really understood "Balance of Terror" yet, with its submarine-type battle in space, but I knew it was my father's favorite from back in his high school days during the show's original run. "The Trouble with Tribbles," and "A Piece of the Action" also quickly became favorites because of their brilliant blend of comedy and high stakes adventure. *Star Trek*, when I was only six or seven, meant everything to me.

I wanted to experience it all. I wanted to fight the Gorn, wanted to know the sensation of beaming down, wanted to sit in the captain's chair. Yes, that chair, with a yeoman bringing me something to sign, and a swiveling view of the bridge of the most beautiful starship I could ever imagine, with a viewscreen showing me the sea of stars through which I sailed. I wanted, more than anything, to be Captain James T. Kirk (except for the occasional day when I wished I was Spock and elongated my ears by attaching clothespins to the tops of them, which was pretty uncomfortable!). I would imagine that my father's car was a shuttlecraft and that we were on our way not to the grocery store, but to a new world to explore; not to visit my grandparents, but to keep an appointment with some aged admirals who would give us new orders for some vital mission. Our house often, in my mind, became the *Enterprise*, and any random object I picked up could transform, in my hands, into a phaser or tricorder. The refrigerator was a food replicator. Yes, I would sometimes tell it what I wanted as I opened the door. Being sent to get something from the basement meant it was time to inspect Engineering. A trip to an outdoor environment, like a walk in the woods with my grandfather or a fishing excursion with Dad meant I was entering territory I'd seen in "The Paradise Syndrome," or "Shore Leave," or, if I chose a more ominous setting, "The Apple." Going to the hardware store meant I had to watch out for the Horta, because, in my mind, it was the mining colony from "Devil in the Dark."

An outside observer might have said I had become obsessed with *Star Trek*, but it would be more accurate to say that I had found a sanctuary. The effect was positive. I endured bullies at school by pretending, privately in my thoughts, that I was Jim Kirk on an alien world, doing my best to navigate through a hostile culture. I found science lessons more interesting than the other kids did, because I knew that science and knowledge were the keys to Starfleet's mission. My love of *Star Trek* made me a better student, made me a more moral person, made me value diversity, for what is life without the wonderful concept of IDIC?

Star Trek was the trigger for many firsts during my childhood. It was the first time I followed a comic book based on a TV series, during the years when DC had the rights. It was the *Star Trek* novels of the time that became the first "adult" books I sought out. My first was *Chain of Attack* by Gene DeWeese. I had two of the Power Records *Star Trek* record and comic sets, "Passage to Moauv," and "The Crier in Emptiness." *Star Trek* was even the first thing I cared enough about to join its official fan club. It was also the first series I ever tried to collect on VHS, and I didn't get very far, since it was sold as single episodes and those tapes were expensive for a kid's allowance in the Eighties! I loved many fictional characters and universes when I was a kid. Star Wars was high on the list, as were Marvel and DC comics, Indiana Jones, and James Bond, among others, but *Star Trek* had the biggest impact. That wonderful, inspiring depiction of the Twenty-third century was where I wanted to be.

Now, let's go back to a time before I discovered the comics and the fan club and the novels, before I had seen any of the movies or owned any of the shows on tape. All I knew at this point was that I loved watching *Star Trek* every Saturday evening and I wanted desperately to be a Starfleet officer, preferably Captain Kirk.

Despite the early impact *Star Trek* had on my imagination and personality, I was still a little boy, and little boys love toys, especially action figures. I already had a bunch of them, mostly Star Wars, because they were everywhere in those days. The toy section of every store was full of Lukes and Leias and Darth Vaders, but, since I knew that *Star Trek* was older, it hadn't occurred to me that it might also be represented in plastic form.

Then, one glorious summer evening, my parents and I happened to stop at Child World, a lesser-known competitor to Toys "R" Us.

Dad and I found a long aisle filled with action figures, vehicles, and playsets. I was thrilled! A large percentage of it was Star Wars, which I loved too, though, I think, just an ounce less than I adored *Star Trek*. There was even a small section of toys from the *Buck Rogers* TV series with Gil Gerard. I don't recall ever seeing those again in person.

But then I saw something else. Something extraordinary! A dream suddenly came true before my eyes. A display of actual *Star Trek* action figures! The image of the *Enterprise* on the package was unmistakable. The faces on the card illustration were familiar (some of them at least), but also strangely different. As it turned out, these figures were for *Star Trek: The Motion Picture*, which I had not seen. I couldn't see it then, for it was out of theaters by a couple years and we were still several years away from our first VCR. But the differences, the duller uniform colors, the slightly older faces, didn't matter to me. I knew who those figures were, and I was overjoyed.

My father saw the look of wonder on my face. He reached out toward the display that I was almost afraid to touch; maybe I thought I would wake up from the dream if I dared make contact with it. He held one of the figures, examined it as if trying to weigh its worth. He looked at me, and I looked back with desperate hope.

"Do you want Kirk and Spock?" he asked.

Now, I was not the kind of kid who often asked for things. I was shy, maybe too polite. I would often say I didn't want something even if I did because I didn't want to inconvenience anyone. But, at that moment, I knew what I had to do.

"And McCoy," I said. And I meant it. "They have to be together. All three of them."

Even at that single-digit age, I knew that Jim, Spock, and Bones belonged together, and I could not bear the thought of leaving that Child World with two of them and not the other. And as the words left my mouth, I was sure I'd crossed a line and would get none of them. But it worked! I went home that night with three of my heroes in my hands. That has to have been one of the happiest nights of my life.

Not long after, I also got the figures of Scotty (it was strange seeing him with a mustache), Decker (I didn't know who he was, not having seen the movie, so he became my Chekov figure), and Ilia, who I really didn't recognize, but she wore a Starfleet insignia, which was good enough for me to find a place for her in the adventures I staged with my new favorite toys.

There was also, at the time, a playset of the bridge of the *Enterprise*, but, as much as I wanted it, my parents just couldn't afford to get me many of those sets to go with my figures, and I understood that. I never held it against them. But I was about to get something even better than that toy version of the bridge. I don't think I quite grasped, at the time, how much better, but I do now, and it makes me almost break down crying at the thought of one of the greatest acts of love and creative generosity I've ever been the recipient of.

While Kirk and Spock were the characters I most often wished I could be, I also had great affection for Dr. McCoy and Scotty. I think part of the reason for this might have been that they were very much like my grandfather, though in different ways. For the first twelve years of my life, until he died, Grandpa was my best friend. He'd grown up on a farm, and his (usually) easygoing manner, supplemented by an occasional jab of sly sarcasm, was quite similar to the personality of Leonard McCoy. And then there was the Scotty side. Grandpa had been taught carpentry and related skills in the Army during World War II and had brought that knowledge home for his long career in construction. The man could build or fix anything! His basement full of tools, always with one project or several in progress, was a wonderland to me, and was probably the closest I'll ever come to feeling like I've entered Montgomery Scott's beloved engine room. There, Grandpa was king of his lower deck castle, and he did things his way, no matter what Captain Grandma upstairs might have thought about it!

And it was there, in that workshop, that my grandfather made one of my dreams come true.

I can't recall if it was my birthday, or Christmas, or if, most likely, it was just another occasion on which Grandpa demonstrated his endless generosity. I didn't know it was coming, I don't know how long it had taken him, and I don't know when he managed to stealthily get some essential measurements, but, one glorious day, Grandpa gave me the *Enterprise*.

It may have been the most beautiful thing I'd ever seen. The bridge of the U.S.S. *Enterprise*, made of wood, painted perfectly, at precisely the size it had to be to provide a home for my figures of her captain and crew.

The base was square, but the components were arranged in a circle, just as they were on TV. Captain Kirk's chair in the center, Spock and Uhura's consoles and seats behind, the helm in front of Kirk, with seats for Sulu and Chekov. Handrails just where they should have been. Everything painted with precision, right down to the turbolift's red doors. All this was of hard, solid wood, cut so beautifully, its colors shining as brightly as if the ship had just begun its mission. And then there was the viewscreen. It was a little bigger, I think, in proportion to the rest than it was in the series, but that was fine with me. The screen was made of a sheet of thin, delicate balsa wood, painted black on the side that faced onto the bridge, with white stars of various sizes speckled randomly across it.

I had never before been given anything like that. I don't know what I said. I hope I was sufficiently grateful. I hope he knew how much I loved it.

When I got home, I immediately put the action figures right where they belonged, each at his or her station. James T. Kirk in the center seat, with Chekov (who was really Decker) and probably some Star Wars figure representing Sulu at navigation and helm, a Fisher Price Adventure People figure (anybody remember those?) playing Uhura at communications, Spock at his usual console, and Scotty and McCoy standing behind their captain. The trick to make them stand was to apply a bit of Silly Putty to the soles of their shoes. Everyone fit. Everyone looked as if they had always been there and always would.

I probably acted out several hundred new episodes of *Star Trek* with that bridge and that crew, adding other figures from other toy lines as aliens or guest stars. So many missions, so many adventures, so many hours of imagination. So much joy.

I got everything I could out of that Enterprise, yet it wasn't until recent years that I realized just what Grandpa had really done for me. You see, there was no internet then to easily look up references. My grandparents didn't have a VCR. Grandpa wasn't the type of man who would go looking for books with pictures of the *Enterprise*. And, most importantly, he didn't even like science fiction. He was too grounded in reality to be a *Star Trek* fan. That's not good or bad, it's just who he was. His TV watching consisted of baseball, westerns, and war movies.

So, based on what I can assume now, in order to make that bridge, and make it look right, down to almost every detail of the layout, the colors, the size of the seats that would hold my action figures (he must have noted the measurements of the figures when I'd been playing in front of him, or called my parents and had them measure the toys), he would have been watching *Star Trek*, a show he probably didn't care for, as many times as he had to in order to make notes about and sketches of the whole bridge. He couldn't pause it either. I wonder how many consecutive Saturday evenings he sat there with his paper and pencil waiting for the moments he needed, snatching the information they provided, then waiting again for the next pertinent bit. The patience that must have taken astounds me.

But the notetaking was only the beginning. Then came the work. Cutting and assembling the whole bridge and every station on it, every chair, every console, and even the handrails, and then painting it in the glorious tones of Sixties television. My head spins just thinking of how long and painstaking the project must have been.

I don't know if my grandfather even really knew what *Star Trek* was about. But he knew that I loved that show. And he knew that he loved me. So, he gave me the *Enterprise*.

Forty years later, I don't know what happened to that handmade Enterprise bridge. It may have been lost the year the river overflowed by the house I grew up in and the basement flooded. I don't know. I wish I still had it.

As I type this, sitting on my desk watching me are James T. Kirk,

Scotty, Decker/Chekov, Fisher Price Uhura, and a Fisher Price nurse who joined in whenever I needed Christine Chapel. Their joints are loose, and their paint is peeling, but they are what I still have of that crew. McCoy and Ilia wore out over time and a lot of play and my mother, I suspect, got rid of them. As for Spock, well, that's my fault! When I saw *The Wrath of Khan*, I went home and dug him a little grave in the backyard. I probably would have gone back to get him in a day or two, since the episodes I created with my toys took place during the original series, but my father mowed the lawn the next day and I hadn't made the grave deep enough, so the role of Spock would from then on be played by a G.I. Joe.

All these years after those Saturday evening episodes, *Star Trek* still inspires me. I may have lost some of the possessions it brought me along my travels, but the memories are all still with me.

Aaron Smith has wanted to tell stories for as long as he can remember, in any form he can. He is the author of more than fifty short stories, including thirteen Sherlock Holmes mysteries, several novels, and a few comic books. For the past several years, his focus has been on music. A songwriter, guitarist, and reluctant singer, he has recorded and released more than twenty-five songs in various genres, from heavy rock to lighter acoustic folk-rock.

THIS IS WHAT HAPPENS WHEN YOU START WATCHING STAR TREK FROM BIRTH

BY KEITH R.A. DECANDIDO

It's all my parents' fault.

See, my parents were—and are—nerds. My parents attended Fordham University, my father from 1964 to 1968, my mother from 1965 to 1969. They met there (amusingly, in a Romantic Literature class), and got married there, in the chapel in Keating Hall, in 1968. Both were avid readers of science fiction and fantasy—which was, indeed, one of the things that attracted them to each other.

And from 1966-1969, both of them religiously watched *Star Trek* on NBC.

I was born in April 1969, so I missed almost all of the show in first-run. In fact, the only episode to air in my lifetime was what turned out to be the series finale, "Turnabout Intruder." That only aired after I was born because its original scheduled airing on March 28, 1969 was preempted by breaking-news coverage of President Eisenhower's death.

However, as I'm sure everyone reading this book knows, the show got new life in syndication, and that's how I watched it. In New York City, the independent station WPIX Channel 11, showed *Star Trek* reruns every weeknight at 6pm.[18]

---

[18] Channel 11 continued to be the exclusive New York home of Trek through to 1995, as it was the station that picked up both *The Next Generation* and *Deep Space Nine* for the New York market, while continuing to show reruns of the original series. It was, therefore, something of a surprise when the United Paramount Network debuted and had as its NYC affiliate WWOR Channel 9, rather than Channel 11, thus putting *Voyager* on a different channel, while fellow upstart network the WB went to Channel 11. Ironically, when UPN and the WB merged into the CW in 2006, it went with Channel 11 as its affiliate, but by that time, *Enterprise* had been canceled and there was no more *Trek* on broadcast television.

So, when I was growing up, my family's routine was pretty straightforward: watch *Star Trek* at 6pm, have dinner after that.

There has never been a time in my life when I wasn't watching *Star Trek* in some form or other. I was utterly captivated by the show. McCoy's snideness. The banter between Sulu and whoever the navigator was that week (mostly Chekov, but also Riley, Stiles, Bailey, and Farrell). Spock's sass. Uhura's singing.

I also adored all the amazing guest stars like Roger C. Carmel ("Mudd's Women," "I, Mudd"), Mark Lenard ("Balance of Terror," "Journey to Babel"), Joan Collins ("The City on the Edge of Forever"), Stanley Adams ("The Trouble with Tribbles"), Diana Muldaur ("Return to Tomorrow," "Is There in Truth No Beauty?"), Gary Lockwood ("Where No Man Has Gone Before"), Ted Cassidy ("What Are Little Girls Made Of?"), and so many more.

As a young heterosexual male, I also had a particularly lurid appreciation of several of the costuming choices, notably the outfits barely worn by Sherry Jackson as Andrea in "What Are Little Girls Made Of?" Diana Ewing as Droxine in "The Cloud Minders," the unidentified women playing the Rigel II chorus girls in "Shore Leave," Angelique Pettyjohn as Shahna in "The Gamesters of Triskelion," Susan Oliver as the Orion dancer in "The Menagerie," Yvonne Craig as Marta in "Whom Gods Destroy," and Mary-Linda Rapelye as Irina Galliulin in "The Way to Eden."

But my favorites were the Klingons. From a very young age, I was captivated by the Klingons, mostly due to two great actors: John Colicos as Kor in "Errand of Mercy"—the first Klingon we ever met—and especially Michael Ansara as Kang in "Day of the Dove." Indeed, these two were of sufficient awesomeness that they were brought back to play their roles multiple times on the spinoff shows[19]. I loved those two in particular because they were worthy opponents to Captain Kirk, giving as good as they got. They were true challenges to our heroes, and they also had tremendous charisma. There were other Klingons who appeared in "Friday's Child," "A Private Little War," "The Trouble with Tribbles," and

---

[19]Colicos, Ansara, and William Campbell, who played Koloth in "The Trouble with Tribbles," all reprised their roles in *Deep Space Nine*'s "Blood Oath." Colicos returned in two more DS9 episodes, "The Sword of Kahless" and "Once More Unto the Breach," while Ansara came back for *Voyager*'s "Flashback."

"Elaan of Troyius," but none of them had the same gravitas as Kor and Kang.

Not all my memories are good ones. For years, the salt vampire in "The Man Trap" and the big green fat guy in "And the Children Shall Lead" gave me nightmares, to the point where I actively avoided watching those two episodes for *years* due to the trauma. (In the latter case, this was hardly a loss, as "And the Children Shall Lead" is definitely a bottom-ten *Trek* episode, not just for the series, but the franchise as a whole.)

I wasn't satisfied with just the TV reruns every night at 6pm, though.

Luckily, there was more to be found. My parents bought the James Blish adaptations of episodes, which was a handy way to experience some of the episodes that I hadn't happened to catch on reruns or hadn't been shown recently.

I started high school in 1982, which wound up being a great time to be a *Trek* fan on several fronts. Personally, while in high school, I met like-minded friends who also enjoyed *Trek*. And this was also the early days of DC's run of *Trek* comics (initially written by Mike W. Barr with art by Tom Sutton and Ricardo Villagran), which debuted in '82, and Simon & Schuster's publishing of *Trek* novels, which had kicked off with Vonda N. McIntyre's *The Entropy Effect* in 1981.

Eventually, I went back and found the Bantam-published novels from the 1970s, but in my high school years it was all about the S&S novels, at first published under their Timescape imprint, later as part of their Pocket Books paperback program. McIntyre's novel remains one of my favorite *Trek* books, and my friends and I were constantly recommending them to each other all throughout our high school years: Howard Weinstein's *The Covenant of the Crown*, Sonni Cooper's *Black Fire* (lurid as hell, but we loved the whole alternate-reality thing), Margaret Wander Bonanno's *Dwellers in the Crucible*, John M. Ford's *The Final Reflection*, Diane Duane's *The Wounded Sky* and *My Enemy, My Ally*, McIntyre's novelizations of *The Wrath of Khan*, *The Search for Spock*, and *The Voyage Home*.

The best thing about finding like-minded contemporaries is that we could all enthuse together about the novels, the comics, and the new movies as they came out. But we could also do things like game together. All my Trekkie[20] friends were also gamers, and that was also when FASA had the license to do a *Trek* role-playing game. It was tremendous fun having our adventures of Captain Thomas Mercier and the *U.S.S. Califia*, and Captain Matteo Kojima and the *U.S.S. Mandela*.

Even as I write these words, I can hear some of you saying, "But what about conventions?" Here's the thing—until college, I never really went to conventions. I hit a few comic-cons in the 1980s (which back then were *just* for comics, with back issues for sale and the occasional writer and artist guest) and went to one Creation show where Leonard Nimoy was a guest that was a huge letdown. (Nimoy's appearance consisted of walking up to the podium, giving a long, rambling talk, during which he stared at an indeterminate point on the back wall, took no questions, and left.)

I mentioned above that my parents were nerds. They were (and still are) fans of science fiction and fantasy, but they never got involved in Fandom (with a capital F) because it never got on their radar.

This, by the way, is why I've always been wary of pronouncements about how "the fans" feel about something based on what they've heard at conventions or, more recently, read about on the Internet. Because there are plenty of people out there—indeed, most of the people out there—who love this stuff without ever once going to a convention. Or buying a fanzine. Or posting on a message board. Or making a Tumblr, Instagram, or Facebook post about it.

At one point in high school, I rather stupidly decided to write my own *Trek* novel, which was a hilariously awful book about Captain Sulu's first mission as captain of the *U.S.S. Mortran*. No, I have no idea what a "Mortran" is. But Sulu was tied with McCoy for my favorite character on the show, mainly because George Takei played him with such a sense of relaxed competence. You always knew you could count on him, whether to fly the ship or be in the landing party or just be a friend. (And occasionally do something silly like play with firearms or something…)

---

[20]The Trekkie/Trekker argument was never a thing in my circle of friends. In fact, I never heard the word "Trekker" until I read about it in a *Best of Trek* volume that collected articles from a fanzine.

I also remembered that in McIntyre's novelization of *The Wrath of Khan*, Sulu was made captain of the *Excelsior*, but was just going on one last mission on the *Enterprise* before taking over. This was based on a scene that was in the shooting script McIntyre based her novel off of but wasn't filmed (or if it was filmed it was never used in any edition of the movie that's been seen). The novelization of *The Search for Spock* dealt with that by having Sulu temporarily removed from command so the events of the movie still worked, and I decided that my *incredibly brilliant* novel would take place after that, with Sulu finally getting the command he deserved. The novel was a bit short, and I wrote three short stories to fill out the space.

It's possible that the 5¼" floppy disks that contained that novel are in a box somewhere in my apartment. It's also possible that they're lost forever. I'm fine either way, as the only part of that awful novel that I think was in any way good was one of the short stories, which was a sequel to "Arena" that had what I think is still a nifty take on the Gorn (basically that they're *extremely* long-lived, and to their mind, the encounter with Kirk on the planet near Cestus III twenty years earlier was only the equivalent of a few days ago by their reckoning).[21]

Of course, eventually I got to write actual *Trek* novels and comic books and short stories, just like the ones I read in high school, though amusingly none of them feature Captain Sulu, nor have I made use of the starship name *Mortran*.

At least not yet.

But *Star Trek* has been an integral part of my life since childhood, progressing well into adulthood, where my fandom has been parlayed into a career writing both for and about Trek.

And it's all my parents' fault.

Keith R.A. DeCandido has been writing novels, short fiction, comic books, reference books, role-playing game material, reviews, rewatches, and commentary about *Star Trek* since 1999. Among his accomplishments are the acclaimed and influential political novel

---

[21] If nothing else, it's, I believe, a more interesting take than what they're doing with the Gorn on *Strange New Worlds*. But that's a subject for a different essay collection…

Articles of the Federation, short fiction in several issues of *Star Trek Explorer* magazine, the oft-reprinted *Alien Spotlight: Klingons* comic book (with art by JK Woodward), *The Klingon Art of War* coffee-table book, material for the *Star Trek Adventures: Klingon Empire Core Rulebook*, reviews of the new Paramount+ shows and rewatches of the classic *Trek* shows for the award-winning webzine Tor.com for the last dozen years, and think-pieces on *Trek* for a variety of essay collections, magazines, and monographs, among them *Entertainment Weekly* and the *Gold Archive* series. He's also written things that have nothing to do with *Star Trek*, as hard to believe as that may be. Find him online at DeCandido.net.

CONFESSIONS OF A STAR TREK NON-FAN FAN

BY PAUL KUPPERBERG

Star Trek didn't loom very large in my life. I had just turned eleven when the series debuted in September of 1966, the perfect age for an idea like *Star Trek* to imprint on an impressionable brain. And I certainly possessed a brain that had proved easily impressed with such things. I seemed to have been indoctrinated in fantastic fiction from birth; I quite literally cannot remember a time when comic books weren't a part of my life. By four or five years old I was already a dyed-in-the-wool fan of the Man of Steel thanks to the 1940s Paramount Superman cartoons and *The Adventures of Superman* syndicated series, both watched originally on a seventeen-inch black and white Philco television. I only found out his costume wasn't gray when my young brain finally connected the blue, red, and yellow on a comic book cover with the monotone depiction on TV.

But I did watch *Star Trek*, if only because it was what was on TV, of which we had the one, situated in the living room. In 1966, viewing wasn't only limited by a lack of options (New York had the three networks, three local stations, and one PBS channel available) but by a dearth of devices to view them on. Most homes had only one television set in a communal space and the entire family watched the same program at the same time.

My parents were fairly liberal in their choice of programming. My father had no use for sitcoms and paid little attention to most hour-longs, but as a teen in the 1930s he'd read the science fiction and fantasy pulps before graduating to the fantastic literature of Jules Verne, H.G. Wells, and H. Rider Haggard, and was a regular viewer of *The Outer Limits* and *The Twilight Zone*.

Mom probably would have preferred watching the Thursday, 8-9pm competition like the highly rated *Bewitched* or *My Three Sons* at eight, or even the new sitcom, That Girl, but my guess is between my father, my brothers, and me, she yielded to the majority and suffered in silence, although not without some cultural pride; as she noted, Captain Kirk *and* Mr. Spock were both Jewish!

Truth is, I have no specific memories of watching the original run of the original series other than recalling thinking several of the later episodes were lame enough to give schlock-TV science fiction producer Irwin Allen a run for his money. And even though there were only three channels, *Star Trek*, unlike the *Enterprise* itself, didn't exist in a vacuum. Never mind all the shows that were already on the air, consider just some of the other prime time programs that debuted alongside it in 1966: *Batman, Mission: Impossible, Family Affair, The Rat Patrol, Tarzan, The Time Tunnel, Daktari, The Green Hornet, It's About Time, That Girl, The Girl from U.N.C.L.E., Mr. Terrific, Iron Horse, T.H.E. Cat, Hawk, Occasional Wife, Love on a Rooftop, Hey Landlord, Run Buddy Run, The Double Life of Henry Phyfe*, to name a relative few, most of which didn't last more than a season or two. I liked science fiction, of course, but at that age most of what I knew came from reading Edgar Rice Burroughs and Isaac Asimov along with the comic book and chintzy video variety of science fiction. And genre wasn't an actual consideration in my viewing choices. To me, "television" itself *was* the genre. The previous year's *Lost in Space* (CBS, 1966–1968) started off with potential, but squandered it all under the inherent cheapness of Irwin Allen TV productions and the shift in focus to the silly Dr. Smith and the Robot show.

But serious science fiction had never fared very well on television. The technology was too primitive to make it look convincing and, anyway, TV was aimed not at sophisticated viewers but at the lowest common denominator to attract the largest audience. A *Twilight Zone* or *Outer Limits* episode here and there aside, the genre seemed to confined to kids shows like *Captain Video and his Video Rangers* (DuMont, 1949–1955) or *The Adventures of Superman* (syndicated,

1952–1959), or as a comedy gimmick for sitcoms like *It's About Time* (CBS, 1966) or *My Favorite Martian* (CBS, 1963–1966), or as window dressing for what was, in the end, traditional TV drama. One of my favorite shows of the time was *The Time Tunnel* (ABC, 1966–1967), a direct contemporary of *Star Trek*, also debuting in September 1966, which dropped its heroes into dramatic situations via time travel instead of a spaceship. But the historic backdrop and science fiction trope had about as much to do with the stories of human drama as history and Western tropes did to the similarly episodic *Wagon Train* (NBC, 1957–1962 and ABC, 1962–1965). They were window dressing on stories that were otherwise interchangeable. Other than the motive for the heroes to be on the move, going weekly from one story to another, shows ranging from *The Fugitive* (ABC, 1963-1967) to *Incredible Hulk* (CBS, 1977–1982) to *Highway to Heaven* (NBC, 1984–1989) and beyond were telling the same sort of stories.

An indication of that interchangeability could even be found in Gene Roddenberry's original pitch to the studios for his series. In an article posted January 3, 2016, *Newsweek* wrote, "When he launched *Star Trek* in 1966, its high concept...was '*Wagon Train* to the Stars': a Western in space."

But Roddenberry fooled them.

The pitch, in TV exec speak, was "*Wagon Train* to the stars."

And, yes, *Star Trek* would be episodic, exploding strange new worlds, seeking out new life and civilizations, etc., but the problems they would find at each new weekly destination weren't the down-to-earth troubles of ordinary people facing adversity. The *Newsweek* article continued, "Roddenberry's model, though, was *Gulliver's Travels*: social, political, even philosophical commentary disguised as adventure. Yet instead of (Jonathan) Swift's savage indignation, Roddenberry had an unsentimental optimism. His earthlings of the future were the same old unstable compounds of good and evil, but they hadn't destroyed themselves, and darned if they'd let ornery aliens push them or anybody else around."

I picked up on none of the subtleties from my initial viewing of the series. I knew that at its best, *Star Trek* was both good television and good science fiction. The forty-five-year-old Roddenberry was a decorated World War II B-17 bomber pilot, former airline pilot, and ex-LAPD cop who found his way into TV as the technical advisor on the *Mr. District Attorney* program. And he took his science fiction, as well as his drama, seriously. What he created in *Star Trek* was fairly sophisticated, right down to the design of the starship Enterprise, a vessel that eschewed the cliché needle-nose rocket and managed to evoke the pop culture concept of the flying saucer without any sense of irony or tongue-in-cheek referencing.

But it was the big picture Roddenberry painted for *Star Trek* that was so impressive, so innovative, so well-constructed, that it was able to draw me in as an adolescent, my brother as a teen, as well as my thirty- and forty-something parents. Because unlike just about any of the other shows that debuted in 1966, or any still running, *Star Trek* expected its audience to accept a fantastic new world in a future that most viewers couldn't begin to conceive. Of course, by 1966 there was nothing alien about the idea of man blasting off into near Earth orbit or even attempting a voyage to the moon in a Mercury or Gemini capsule atop a needle-nose rocket propelled by liquid hydrogen and oxygen, but no serious, adult entertainment program had ever posited a civilization that had spread out among the stars, traveling at faster than light speeds in giant space battleships propelled by...dilithium crystals?

Every new TV series requires a certain amount of "world building," even if it's as simple as the one inhabited by *That Girl*'s Anne Marie (Marlo Thomas): young actress, a New York City apartment, determined to make it in show business, surrounded by boyfriend, agent, parents, neighbors, and guest-stars. Even *Lost in Space*, which quickly careened off into the uncharted universe, was launched from a familiar, more or less contemporary world and was informed by the then current excitement of space exploration. Sending the Robinsons off, one might add, aboard the *Jupiter 2*, a ship that made no attempt to hide its clichéd flying saucer origin.

But *Star Trek* wasn't just setting a scene or building a world; it was building an entire universe. One in which humans and aliens coexisted across the cosmos, sometimes peacefully, sometimes not. One where communications was achieved through small, handheld wireless devices and food replicators, transporters, and computers (!) were as routine as refrigerators, automobiles, and manual typewriters were to us.

Like *The Twilight Zone* and *The Outer Limits*, *Star Trek* used its science fiction label as cover for the often-radical sociopolitical ideas (well, "radical" for the bland, whitewashed social politics of the mid-1960s) it advocated. A serious story about racial equality in America was easily masked from (or credibly ignored by) network censors when hidden under Frank Gorshin and Lou Antonio's half-white/half-black alien make-up in season three's "Let That be Your Last Battlefield."

Despite the familiarity of its "workplace family," the core crew of characters brought together by the circumstances of their profession, even *Star Trek*'s casting was radical. Though still predominantly white and male like most television of the day, the addition of George Takei's Hikaru Sulu and Nichelle Nicols' Uhura as members of the Enterprise's hierarchy made critics and fans alike sit up and take notice. Even the inclusion of (American actor) Walter Koenig's Russian helmsman Chekov at the height of US/USSR Cold War tensions was a slap at the current orthodoxy, positing a future where the nations of Earth would come together to conquer space as well as the dark forces of Communism.

In retrospect, I can't tell you what I took from *Star Trek* on my original viewing of it. My critical skills ranged from "I like it" to "this stinks," and were too undeveloped to recognize subtly, let alone subtext. The show went into limited syndication on, among other stations, WPIX-TV in New York where I lived not long after finishing its network run. According to a contemporary Associated Press article ("Cult Fans, Reruns Give *Star Trek* an Out of This World Popularity," July 3, 1972), *Star Trek* had become "the show that won't die" and was running in more than one-hundred cities in the US and sixty countries abroad.

By the time *Star Trek* ended its network run in 1969, I had entered a phase of youthful science fiction snobbery. Though still a consumer of "old school" SF, I had discovered the Science Fiction Book Club and as one of my selections for the "six books for $1" initial offer, I chose *Dangerous Visions* (Doubleday 1967), Harlan Ellison's groundbreaking New Wave anthology, and my definition of the genre changed overnight. I lost all taste for lightweight TV SF and found network shows like *The Six Million Man* (ABC, 1973–1978) and *The Bionic Woman* (ABC, 1976–1978) embarrassingly silly and unwatchable. *Battlestar Galactica* (1978) and *Logan's Run* (1977–1978) and imports like *Space: 1999* (1975–1977) and *Blake's 7* (1978–1981) felt tired and derivative. My taste had changed, I stopped watching television science fiction and, by the early-1980s, lost interest in the genre in print as well except for the occasional nostalgic rereading of old favorites.

But I never quite abandoned *Star Trek*.

I may not have marked my *TV Guide* to catch every showing of the show in syndication, but when I came across an episode channel surfing, I would always stop and watch it through to the end. It was, like the earlier *The Adventures of Superman*, comfort food for me. I was old enough to recognize the subtleties that had once gone over my head, and I appreciated that, in the first two seasons at least, the producers had often hired bona fide science fiction authors to write scripts, including Robert Bloch, David Gerrold, Richard Matheson, Norman Spinrad, Theodore Sturgeon, and, most famously, the aforementioned Ellison.

Like *Batman*, which premiered the same year, *Star Trek* had a relatively short initial run that made a lasting impact on pop culture. Batman's onomatopoeic "Pow! Zap! Bam!" became media shorthand for anything related to comic books, and references to *Star Trek* and its "five-year mission…to boldly go where no man has gone before" was almost sure to turn up in mass media stories about rocketry or space exploration.

But it was that very mass-market appeal that was part of what kept drawing me back to the 1960s *Star Trek* and the subsequent TOS films. Like those today who call themselves "comic book fans" based on solely on watching the films but seldom if ever reading a comic book, the idea and execution of *Star Trek* was so compelling, it made even those who only ever watched the program and couldn't tell Alfred Bester from Ray Bradbury become "science fiction fans." The appeal was in the writing and the cast who spoke the words. The dynamics between the characters in all its myriad permutations was what brought the show to life. Even in episodes where the science fiction was dubious or the message weak or neglected, the bond between Kirk and Spock and the crew came through. We didn't need to wait until Spock's dying declaration in *Star Trek II: The Wrath of Khan* (Paramount, 1982) to know that they always had been—and always shall be—friends. The warmth and genuine camaraderie projected on the screen kept *Star Trek* on the air in syndication and fueled seven movies over fifteen years (not to mention the countless sequels and spin-offs in the thirty years since), helping as much as anything to mainstream credible science fiction for general audiences.

The eleven-year-old who watched those original episodes couldn't have dreamed that *Star Trek* would one day grow into a permanent fixture of the pop culture landscape—and, yes, the corporate bottom line as well. Maybe *Star Trek* didn't get to complete its original five-year mission, but the fact that it lives on fifty-plus years later, and that this TV science fiction skeptic still stops to watch episodes when they pop up on the oldies channel shows that it may be mission accomplished after all. In more ways than one.

Among his thousand+ comic book scripts for DC Comics, Archie Comics, Marvel Comics, and dozens of books for publishers including Crazy 8 Press, Grosset & Dunlap, Kensington, and Rosen Books, **Paul Kupperberg** includes two issues of DC's *Star Trek* comics, a novella for the *Star Trek: SEC* franchise from Pocket Books, and the 1982 Marvel Comics *Crazy Magazine* parody of *Star Trek III: The Wrath of Khan*. You can follow him at PaulKupperberg.net, on Facebook and Twitter, and at Crazy8Press.com.

THE TAPESTRY OF TREK

BY ANDREW LEYLAND

I wasn't a fan of *Star Trek*.

Now I know what you're thinking and you're right; "Not an auspicious start to an essay about *Star Trek* memories!" but it's the truth, I wasn't a fan. As with most kids my age, my heart belonged to *Star Wars*.

However, I was a fan of genre TV generally, particularly if it was sci-fi or comic book related. *The Six Million Dollar Man*, *The Bionic Woman*, and *The Man from Atlantis* all popped up on the UK TV schedules, later followed by actual comic book adaptations, *The Amazing Spider-Man, Wonder Woman*, and my favorite, *The Incredible Hulk*. Cartoons also fuelled my genre obsession and again, I liked things like *Battle of the Planets* which, in the wake of *Star Wars*, had been retrofitted into a space adventure series. I tuned in every week to *Doctor Who* and *Blake's 7*, which tended to be referred to as, "the British *Star Trek*," presumably by people who hadn't actually watched either show.

I was, however, *aware* of *Star Trek*. My nan enjoyed the adventures of the Starship Enterprise, and I would watch along with her. I had also seen adverts for *Star Trek: The Motion Picture* in the back of old comics but probably thought it was another *Star Wars* knock-off like *The Black Hole* or *Battlestar Galactica*.

As a British kid, I was also quite confused by *Star Trek*. Most imported genre fare tended to air on the BBC's main rival, ITV, and of the foreign shows mentioned above, only *Wonder Woman* and *Battle of the Planets* were on the BBC. ITV aired the cooler American stuff as well as the Gerry Anderson programmes, tales of undersea derring-do like *Stingray*, earthbound adventures like *Captain Scarlet* and *UFO* and, another favorite, the crew of Moonbase Alpha encountering the weirdly horrific every week on *Space 1999*. To my young mind, the BBC airing *Star Trek* at all seemed somewhat odd, although they did also air *The Dukes of Hazzard*, so it wasn't all highbrow Shakespeare adaptations and classical concerts.

Now, yes, *Trek* ended up being a cut above most of the shows mentioned above, but I'm pretty sure that without *Doctor Who*, we may never have seen *Trek* on the BBC at all.

What? Really?

Yes. Really.

See, by 1969, the venerable Time Lord was showing his age and the BBC weren't sure they were going to continue with the series. Other ideas were bandied about; a series based upon the stories of Jules Verne or a revived version of the successful 1950s series, *Quatermass*, but neither gained any traction. With literally nothing else ready to go, the BBC ordered a stay of execution for *Doctor Who*.

So where does *Star Trek* come into this?

Well, with the decision to retain the services of The Doctor, certain changes were made to that show's format; firstly, there would no longer be forty-four episodes a year, rather only twenty-six. The savings in money would be applied to the filming, which would now be in color and on location for a few episodes. In addition, *Doctor Who* would no longer debut in the autumn schedules, rather be held back to launch the New Year schedules, so to fill in the shortfall, the BBC would need a new series to plug the gap.

Enter, *Star Trek*, a show seemingly tailor made for this purpose.

There is evidence that the BBC had *Star Trek* on the shelf for a while before actually airing it. The series had been appearing in the *Joe 90* comic, a tie-in to the Gerry Anderson series of the same name, since January 1969 so, by the time it actually aired on the BBC on the 12th July 1969, the nation's kids were already somewhat familiar with the adventures of the crew of the *Enterprise*, even if they thought the commander was Captain Kurt! The creators of the comic strip had obviously never seen the series, after all it hadn't aired yet! A spelling error therefore gave us a different commander of the *Enterprise*.

Nevertheless, the BBC did start airing the show and to lessen confusion, did they follow the US transmission?

No, that would be too obvious, I grant you.

So, possibly they would choose to air the series in production order, a sequence that does make more sense.

That would be far too easy.

No, the BBC chose to air *Star Trek* in an order best described as "haphazard." Sure, the first episode transmitted was the pilot episode, "Where No Man Has Gone Before," but that was followed up with "The Naked Time" and then "The City on The Edge of Forever." Despite the bizarre order, the series proved immensely popular, and the BBC stayed pretty true to the *Star Trek* cause, with regular airings from its debut in 1969, through to 1982, skipping only 1977.

And it's thanks to these reruns, I became a fan.

Partially.

In February 1984, DC Comics launched their new tie-in comic series based upon *Star Trek* and I was instantly attracted to the George Perez cover. I shelled over my twenty-five pennies to purchase the book and was instantly intrigued; the characters were older, the crew different, and Mr Spock was conspicuous by his absence. The fact that this wasn't a retread of the TV show made it more compelling and any questions I had were more than ably answered in the letters page by editor Robert Greenberger. I read the first four issues, the space operatics and character dynamics reeling me in. This replacement character for Spock, Saavik, was particularly intriguing and I looked forward to future issues.

Then, on 26th June 1984, just over a week after my twelfth birthday, the BBC started a new rerun of *Star Trek* but, for the first time, they were showing the series in its original broadcast order. For whatever reason, I did not see the first episode, "The Man Trap," but I did see the next one, "Charlie X," which aired the following week on 3rd July 1984. I enjoyed it and was interested in seeing where it went.

Star Trek had got its hook in my mouth.

I dutifully tuned in to the next episode, "Where No Man Has Gone Before."

Star Trek reeled me in.

This episode, as with the comics, showed a different crew with only a few familiar faces. Even at that young age, I was savvy enough to know this episode had to take place before the one I'd seen last week. Time had clearly passed between the episodes and the comics, but even in the time frame of the series itself, things had changed. How long was the crew like this? When did Dr. McCoy come aboard? He was here last week but this week, the doctor was named Boyce. The ship also looked different somehow. The uniforms were only gold and blue, there were no red shirts. Spock was even more alien and had a tendency to grin and Kirk's closest friend was someone called Gary Mitchell. Were there other stories to tell with this version of the crew?

Forget being hooked and reeled in; *Star Trek* had landed me!

I didn't know it at the time, but this was the moment I stopped being a "viewer" and became a "fan." I devoured the next sequence of episodes before I almost lost the show. After only six weeks the BBC changed the time slot! This would become a regular occurrence and was extremely annoying. Despite this, the BBC stuck with the rescreening. Sure, like the Enterprise in the wormhole, it bounced around a bit, changing times and even days, but it was always there.

Somewhere.

On 4th September 1984, the BBC reached a rerun of the only two-part episode of the series run, "The Menagerie."

Can open, worms everywhere!

The *Enterprise* was more than fourteen years old and had once had another Captain, Christopher Pike and, Mr Spock excepted, another crew! The scope for new adventures just cracked open like an egg dropped from a four-story building. Who was Pike? Who were these other crewmembers? What happened to them?

I was agog. I didn't know at the time that this was repurposed footage from an earlier, rejected pilot episode, I just wanted more.

And I got it!

The day before, in fact. On the 3rd September 1984, ITV beat the BBC to the punch and aired the television premiere of *Star Trek: The Motion Picture*. I had recorded this televisual event, seeing the much maligned and, IMO, highly underrated entry in the series for the first time. Kirk was older! He was no longer captain, that role taken by a new character named Will Decker. Spock was AWOL & McCoy had to be drafted!

What was occurring?

As a fan of Marvel Comics, I was aware of and understood the ever-unfolding narrative text, but this was something new. The characters were all at different stages of their lives across multiple projects and seeing it all unfold like this, with the same actors in the roles across many years, was revelatory. *Star Trek* was now more than a TV show, it was mythology!

Having been hooked, reeled in, and landed, *Star Trek* now had me cooking on the grill.

The voyages of the *Enterprise* were like a vast tapestry, running over many years. This is probably why the destruction of the *Enterprise* in the newest film, *Star Trek III: The Search for Spock*, gutted me, competently handled though it was. If there was one thing I'd gleaned from all this *Star Trek*king it was that these were the voyages of the Starship *Enterprise*. You could replace the captain and crew, but the *Enterprise* was a beautiful lady and we loved her. Without her, there *was* no going boldly.

I continued to devour the weekly adventures, spurred on by the realization there were extra sources of information such as comics and novels. I wanted more so I sought it out. For the first time, I discovered comics specialty shops existed. I found one in Manchester, the nearest city to where I lived. It was called Odyssey 7, and entering it for the first time, I swear I heard choirs of angels. The series was merely a springboard for other adventures and stories, and I wanted to read them all.

By December 1984, the BBC reruns had reached the end of Season One of the original show although the promise of airing them in the correct order had been somewhat abandoned. For some reason, "The Squire of Gothos" and "The Return of the Archons" both aired after "The City on the Edge of Forever," but before "Operation—Annihilate!" At least they were part of the first season. "Miri" had been skipped over again due to its unsuitability for an early evening audience. I would have to rent *that* episode on video.

For Christmas that year, my grandparents had bought me a copy of *The Star Trek Compendium* by Allan Asherman. It was here I'd learned *why* "The Menagerie" and "Where No Man Has Gone Before" had felt so different—they were the series pilots! I've already mentioned that one of the things that I quickly glommed onto was the world building and the character backstories, and I felt vindicated in my feeling that "Where No Man Has Gone Before" and "The Menagerie" felt different to the surrounding episodes. This book, like Clarrisa, explained it all. The answers were, to coin a phrase, "fascinating."

So exciting, so new. All this information, now at my fingertips. I could see which episodes I'd missed, and which were still to come. To twelve-year-old me, there was no such thing as a bad episode of *Star Trek*, just new adventures to devour.

The characters were vibrant and likeable, but my favourite was Captain Kirk. He seemed like a solid bloke. Dependable and smart. Somewhat of a worrier in private. He'd confide in Dr McCoy about his concerns but to the crew, he was clearly in charge. If people died, Kirk mourned. He was well read, a thinker but a fighter when necessary. I never saw him as a rule breaker or a maverick. He had a wide latitude to fulfil his brief but that's because he was at the edge of what was known. He couldn't go and ask Starfleet for advice every week because a decision had to be made there and then. Lives depended on it. He demonstrated that it was fine to listen to other people and their opinions. No man was an island. The nature of '60s US TV meant he was never allowed to really develop. One week, the love of his life died, the following week he lost his brother. The week after that, he was fine. Character exploration like this was left to the extracurricular media. This was where US TV differed to UK TV. Gan's death in *Blake's 7* informed Blake's every decision to the end of the season. Kirk just got on with it.

As I got further into the show, I started taping the episodes. My grandad had bought a video recorder, our first, in the summer of 1982. This was doubly exciting to me as it meant we had a video recorder for the first TV airing of *Star Wars* in October that year. This also meant that by the time this rerun of *Star Trek* began, we had about six video tapes which I dutifully filled with episodes to re-watch. To this day, episodes I had on tape, I can still quote almost verbatim. "Shore Leave" was an early favorite, probably because I managed to stop it being taped over by this Sunday's rugby match for a good long time. I recall the BBC's tape snapped after the teaser for 'Return of the Archons' meaning the title of the episode was lost. It would be years later before I learned why; the BBC, not being a commercial venture, had recut the episodes so the opening titles aired first. "Now on BBC1, the crew of the *Enterprise* take us on another, *Star Trek!*" the announcer would state before we launched directly into the opening titles. Then we would see the teaser, followed by a clumsy edit, before the title of the episode would be seen and Act One would begin. On "Return of the Archons," apparently the Sellotape that stuck the episodes together, snapped! I learned of other edits; anytime an episode went to a commercial break with a dramatic pause, and returned to almost the same place, the BBC would trim the scenes to make a seamless run.

I say, "seamless"!

Still, this made sense in episodes like, "The Paradise Syndrome" which features a lengthy reprise of information post adverts that, when aired on the BBC, would make the viewer feel like they themselves had fallen into a space/time warp. I felt that way on 13th February 1985. The series had nestled into an early evening time slot, perfectly scheduled to get the kids and the adults. But, on this date, following an airing of "Who Mourns for Adonais," the BBC's reruns, ceased.

They couldn't stop now!

The best was yet to come!

And come it did.

When *Star Trek* returned in September, an eternity as a kid, it would now be on BBC2 in its regular time slot of 6pm on Thursday evenings. It would run until the middle of Season 3 before the series took a summer break. "Spectre of the Gun" aired on 10th April

1986 whilst over on ITV, the British Television Premiere of *Star Trek II: The Wrath of Khan* took place on 14th May 1986. This was a soothing balm whilst I waited for the final episodes to air, sadly ruined by ridiculous and heavy-handed editing. Unlike the BBC, ITV *is* a commercial venture and they aired *Trek II* in a two-hour slot from 8pm until 10pm. Sans commercials, the film is 113 minutes and at that time ITV aired ten minutes of commercials per hour.

You can see the problem!

To fit into this slot, ITV needed to cut about thirteen minutes of the film and so they dutifully set about the movie with a pair of rusty shears, hacking away at it. Gone was the scene where Kirk approaches the *Enterprise* in drydock, the film instead coming back from commercials as he boards the *Enterprise*. Then, a loud pop signified the cutting of the *Enterprise* leaving drydock, leaping straight from Saavik and Spock's subtitled conversation to Space Station *Regula 1*. Also missing, the Ceti Eels burrowing into Chekov and Tyrell's ears and, most bizarrely, Kahn's line of dialogue, "I shall avenge you!" It's a testament to the overall enjoyment of the film that it survived this hatchet job and still emerged as a cracking yarn.

The series returned to BBC2 on the 4th September 1986 with "Day of the Dove" and ended with "Turnabout Intruder" on 18th December 1986. A weird and out of place additional rerun of "The Galileo Seven" aired on 30th December 1986. Once again, the BBC had omitted screening, "Whom Gods Destroy," "Plato's Stepchildren," and "The Empath" due to reasons of unsuitability. These last three episodes would not be aired on any previous airing of the show and, along with "Miri," which was only ever screened once on 2nd December 1970, would not be seen on the BBC until 1993. I had a few episodes on numerous video tapes but the thrill of getting a new (to me) episode every week was over.

The feeling would be somewhat replicated starting the 16th November 1987 when CIC Video would release, in full, the original pilot "The Cage" with an introduction from Gene Roddenberry. They would follow this with monthly releases of two episodes to one video tape and I bought them all at £9.99 a tape. Looking back, this was a ridiculous amount of money but back then, it was the only way I could amass a complete and uncut collection of the original show. I got my money's worth though, re-watching the tapes over and over.

By this time however, *Star Trek* wasn't the only game in town, Roddenberry having launched *Star Trek: The Next Generation* in autumn 1987. The voyages of the Starship *Enterprise* would continue into the 24th century and beyond.

In retrospect this was probably my key time as a *Star Trek* fan. The comics were expanding on the characters in between the films, the movies were coming out regularly and I had been watching the series weekly, as it was meant to be seen. Thanks to these comics, I was introduced to the novels, which featured great work by Diane Duane, Ann Crispin, Vonda McIntyre, Howard Weinstein, John M Ford and even people who had written for the series like David Gerrold and Dorothy Fontana. These comics and novels enhanced the experience of discovering the old show and drinking deep from the well. *The Next Generation* would only expand upon the history of the Enterprise, eventually giving us an Enterprise B and C and two new captains, John Harriman, and Rachel Garrett.

Looking back, a lot of this was serendipity. That the BBC would start a rerun, just as DC would publish a licensed comic, just as the films started coming out on a regular basis, just as I turned twelve, the golden age for sci-fi—it was like an alignment of stars. Taking *The Next Generation* into account, which started when I was in high school, my ten years of core Trekdom, 1984-1994, covered nearly a century of stories. After *The Next Generation* finished, I was never quite as devout. The thing I loved, the continuing voyages of the *Enterprise*, were lost. *Deep Space Nine* continued the future history, but once that finished, it was over. *Voyager* was off in the Delta Quadrant, *Enterprise*, *Strange New Worlds*, and *Discovery* were prequels, and the films rebooted. The voyages of the Starship *Enterprise* were over and remained so until 2023 and the third season of *Picard*. Hopefully, we'll see more of the *Enterprise* under the command of Captain Seven going forward but my heart will always belong to the original.

Because these *are* the voyages of the Starship *Enterprise*, its ongoing mission; to explore strange new worlds, to seek out new life and new civilizations.

To go boldly, where none have gone before.

Andrew Leyland is a lifelong fan of comics, genre TV, books, and film. He has had articles published in *Back Issue Magazine*, and *Den of Geek*. He is a podcaster, contributing to non-award winning cross generational show, *Hey Kids, Comics!* with his son Micheal, *The Overlooked Dark Knight* with Michael Bailey and his pop culture meanderings, *The Palace of Glittering Delights*. When he grows up, he wants to be a Hawaiian Based Private Investigator.

Andrew would like you to know the website http://space-doubt.blogspot.com/2014/10/star-trek-on-bbc-part-one.html was invaluable in checking the airdates and rerun schedule for *Star Trek* on the BBC, as was the BBC Genome project.

THE ENTERPRISE INFLUENCE

BY MICHAEL A. GORDON

"Space...the Final Frontier."

I was born in November 1968, seven months before the first man took that "small step" on to the moon. While eyes were glued to television screens all across the globe, I have no actual memory of watching that historic event as it happened. To be fair, I was working on taking my own small steps on this planet. Furthermore, I do not recall viewing any of the space missions that followed over the next few years. It's not that I wasn't interested, I just had other things to deal with such as potty training, learning to speak, and discovering what foods did not make me spit up. However, even without actively witnessing NASA's activities, the excitement of space exploration still permeated my childhood. Every boy I knew wanted to be an astronaut, including me. Everywhere you looked there were space toys, space cereal, space drinks, space candy, space songs, space movies, and space television shows.

"These are the voyages of the Starship *Enterprise*."

Two years before I was born, the original series of *Star Trek* made its debut. Although I was alive during the third and final season, I have no direct memories of watching any of the episodes as they originally aired on NBC (though there is an eerie coincidence that I'll get to shortly). My parents did not watch the series and I believe I can safely say that even after all this time, neither my mother nor my father have watched an entire episode of any incarnation of *Star Trek*.

I am a proud member of the last batch of the "first TV generation," those who grew up with an extremely limited number of over-the-air broadcast channels. I believe I and many of my contemporaries were the first to be raised on *Sesame Street*, and the first major network prime time series that caught my attention was *The Six Million Dollar Man*. However, many of my favorite shows to this day are those that were produced in the mid to late sixties and were syndicated on UHF channels in the early seventies. Thanks to Boston independent stations WSBK-TV 38 and WLVI 56, I was introduced in particular to *The Addams Family*, *Batman*, and *Get Smart*, and each continues to resonate in my personality in some form. However, there has been no other force majeure of fiction that has influenced my life as much as *Star Trek*.

"Its five-year mission, to explore strange new worlds, to seek out new life and new civilizations."

The earliest episode of *Star Trek* I recall seeing via syndication was "The Tholian Web." (The aforementioned eerie coincidence—it originally premiered on network television a few days after I was born). A suspenseful adventure crafted by Judy Burns and Chet Richards of space anomalies, spider-like aliens, and mutinous tension among the crew dialed up to eleven. But for me, the striking image of the ghost-like Captain Kirk in a spacesuit silently calling out to his crew as he is trapped between dimensions was enough to haunt me for decades. I still get chills thinking about it.

I think it is safe to say that overall, the unique visuals of *Star Trek* stimulated my eyes like sugar tickled my taste buds. I became addicted to the bold colors of the Starfleet uniforms, the clean lines of the interiors, the exotic alien costumes, the otherworldly set designs, the marvelous props, and of course, the attractive actors. Standing out among everything else, however, was the USS *Enterprise* 1701. Oh, how I loved the design of that ship! I was familiar with real life spacecraft as well as supposedly fictional flying saucers, but the original Constitution-class Federation flagship was the most beautiful vessel I had ever seen. I came to later realize that the form of the *Enterprise* has no practical value for real life space travel and yet, it is still difficult for me to imagine trekking around the universe in anything else. In an early act of hubris, I did try to replicate the beauty and elegance of the Enterprise by completing a build of an AMT model kit at some point in the Seventies. Much like Icarus whose wings were melted by the sun due to poor construction, my attempt did not survive much past completion.

While it was the style of *Star Trek* that drew me in, it was the substance that ultimately satisfied me and kept me wanting more. I may not be able to recount a single NASA mission from the Seventies, but I can recall several episodes of the series that thrilled me in a variety of ways. Little did I know it at the time, but not only was I being entertained, I was also being educated on a number of levels. Sure, there were some not so subtle morality plays that reflected the then current events. I was also discovering science facts and theories that were much more interesting than anything presented in my classroom. And perhaps most impressively, I was understanding that folks of different backgrounds, ethnicities, and personal beliefs could successfully work together. That "Infinite Diversity in Infinite Combinations" was not just a logical philosophy, but one that encouraged truth and beauty. When some folks claim that all they ever really needed to know in life, they learned from *Star Trek*, they'll get no argument from me.

For me personally, *Star Trek* also presented in full color some seriously advanced lessons in storytelling. I took up reading at a very early age and devoured any books I could get my tiny little hands on; Little Golden Books, Dr. Suess, Maurice Sendak, and countless comics. I loved stories, and I especially enjoyed ones that had cliff hangers (*The Monster at the End of This Book* was my favorite of them all). This fondness for serialized storytelling was perfectly applicable to the multi-act format of the average television show. And *Star Trek* was far above average, especially when it came to a suspenseful end to each act highlighted by the best music cues ever orchestrated. The only series that could compete was *Batman* and that was largely because the producers were adapting successful page-turners from the comic books and had very campy narration.

Many television shows at the time were extremely limited in scope—one note melodramas or single joke sitcoms. Once in a great while, you'd find a clever satire or the occasional double entendre (if it could get past the censors). But while *Star Trek* was a show that most saw as mere science fiction fantasy, it could contain many kinds of stories under that umbrella. Action-packed ones such as "Arena" and "Amok Time" were more than just your typical fights, these battles were deeper and more meaningful. Lighter fare, such as "The Trouble with Tribbles" and "A Piece of the Action," had humor but the laughs were never at the expense of the series. I was successfully creeped out by "Dagger of the Mind" and "Wolf in the Fold." My young heart was moved by "The City on the Edge of Forever" and "For the World Is Hollow and I Have Touched the Sky." My mind was blown with the science fiction concepts of "The Doomsday Machine" and "Mirror, Mirror." I was on the edge of my recliner at the intensity of "Balance of Terror" and "Errand of Mercy." All were well-executed implementations of other genres and some of my favorite episodes of the series.

The stories were so consistently powerful that I craved more and looked to other media to get my *Star Trek* fix. Of course, I tuned in to the animated series as often as I could. I also enjoyed the Gold Key comics, the Power records, the original "expanded universe" novels (my favorites were *The Klingon Gambit* by Robert E. Vardeman and *Spock Messiah* by Theodore R. Cogswell and Charles A. Spano Jr.), and even the episodic novelizations by James Blish and Alan Dean Foster. However, the book that made the most impact on me was *The Making of Star Trek* by Stephen E. Whitfield. Not only did it contain a comprehensive behind-the-scenes look at the making of the series I loved so much, but it also provided insight as to how I could participate as well. After all, the tagline on the top of the front cover was "The Book on How to Write for TV!" Thus began my lifelong ambition to write for *Star Trek*.

"To boldly go where no man had gone before."

Even before I read Whitfield's book, I was creating *Star Trek* stories of my own. There was not a lot of *Star Trek* licensed merchandise available back in the Seventies, certainly not in comparison to today's standards. Nevertheless, I tried to get anything *Trek*-related I could find and afford. Along with the novels, comics, and records, I had a couple of the models and a Remco disc-shooting phaser. I would have loved to participate in some live action role-play (as it's called now), but sadly I did not have many friends that shared my passion, and my younger sister was reluctant to be referred to as a "Klingon" and have her eye shot out. But who needs living breathing life-sized human beings to play with when you can have miniature plastic action figures? Mego to the rescue! (When much later Playmates would obtain the *Star Trek* figure license, I thought it was a very on-the-nose company name.)

My action figures were my most prized possessions. The members of G.I. Joe's Adventure Team (even the ones with Kung-Fu grip), Big Jim, and The Six Million Dollar Man were all set aside for the eight-inch figurines of Captain Kirk and Mister Spock, as well as Batman, Robin, Spider-Man, Green Goblin, Joker, and Cornelius from *Planet of the Apes*. And they all could be played with and stored in the exquisite and inventive USS *Enterprise* Playset, in my opinion, one of the best playsets ever created. Sure, it wasn't very screen accurate, yet it was extremely playable and very durable. My figures took that transporter chamber for a spin so many times, yet it never broke (certainly much more reliable as the transporter on the series).

Sadly, my *Enterprise* Playset, as well as the figures stored inside, has been lost to time. What I wouldn't give to be reunited with them! And what I wouldn't give to slingshot around the sun or visit the Guardian of Forever to get a glimpse of younger me orchestrating epic adventures featuring those Megos. I certainly put some wear and tear on those figures! However even before they could be completely beaten, battered, and beyond repair, they were all too soon to be set aside to join my other larger figures for a much smaller cast of characters courtesy of Kenner's three-and-three-quarter inch *Star Wars* line.

Star Wars and the many space adventure movies and shows that followed broke the *Star Trek* spell I was under, at least for a while. The last real significant *Star Trek* original series event for me happened in June 1982 when Channel 56 aired a special screening of "Space Seed" promoting *Star Trek II: The Wrath of Khan*. I was a little familiar with the episode, but I did not believe it warranted a big screen sequel. However, rewatching it soon before I saw the movie prepared me for a special experience that would enhance my feelings for both. It definitely added to the excitement of seeing the *Enterprise* crew face Khan again. As I waited in the theater lobby to be seated for the film, folks from the previous screening were leaving and passed me with tears in their eyes. I knew I was in for an intense experience! *Star Trek II: The Wrath of Khan* exceeded all my expectations, and it still ranks as one of my overall favorite films and my viewing of it gets better as I get older. The dialog of that movie made such an impression that nearly every day some random line comes to my mind. Particularly popular phrases include "He tasks me. He tasks me and I shall have him." "What if they went nowhere?" and "There she is!" However, as much as I enjoyed the film, *Star Trek II* did not bring tears to my eyes when I saw it for the first time in the theater. No, it was a particularly explosive scene in *Star Trek III: The Search for Spock* released a few years later that did that. As I witnessed the beloved *Enterprise* meet its disastrous fate, I echoed Kirk when he uttered, "My god Bones, what have I done?"

I have enjoyed the *Star Trek* franchise in varying degrees over the years that followed, but only occasionally have I come across something that approaches the equivalent to my experience with the original series. I've been fortunate to meet and express my appreciation to many folks who helped make the show and each one I've encountered has been gracious and good-natured. One of the most extraordinary and cherished experiences I've ever had was touring the sets of a *Star Trek* fan film that were a detailed replica of the original *Enterprise* interiors. Walking down the corridors, standing on the transporters, seeing sickbay, engineering, and the crew quarters was incredibly surreal, but the pièce de resistance was sitting in the captain's chair on the bridge. It was truly a dream come true!

And speaking of dreams coming true, for a long time it was a primary goal of mine to write for *Star Trek* in some capacity. To contribute in some small way to the franchise that has had such a positive influence on my life. I have indeed made many attempts. However, I came to realize that writing or even being at the creative helm of *Star Trek* would not ultimately be true to what the original series taught me. I would be continuing Gene Roddenberry's heritage as opposed to creating my own. And that's what I have been working on ever since—a legacy of my own.

Not that I would ever turn down an opportunity to work on *Star Trek*. If anyone reading this can influence the current powers that be, I'm sure I could give it some time. Though in many ways sharing these memories is the ideal tribute to something that has meant so much to me, a reminder of the spark that ignited the flame in me over fifty years ago. To boldly go.

Michael Gordon is a writer, publisher, and podcaster. His creator-owned comic, *Tiki Zombie*, has been running for over a decade. He has also worked on various other books including *The Untold Origins of Invisible Scarlet O'Neil*, *Crypto Zo*, *Strong Will* (with the award-winning author Bobby Nash), and the *Earth Station One: Tales of the Station* and upcoming *Dragon Tales* anthology series. Michael can also be heard saying, "Howdy!" on the weekly *Earth Station One* podcast, as well as a few other shows, mostly on the ESO Network. Visit him online at newlegendmike.com.

BOLDLY BITS AND PIECES

BY SORELLA SMITH

I don't have many memories before April 8, 1980.

That date bears no specific significance to *Star Trek*, only to me. Of the probably less than thirty recollections I have before that date, however, more than one of them relates directly to *Star Trek*. I remember seeing the first movie on the day it hit theaters. Related to the original series, two events stand out clearly for me.

I am willing to bet, and believe I felt then, that I may have been the only kid in Greenville, Mississippi, who wanted to be Dr. Leonard McCoy for Halloween in 1978. It wasn't a last-minute thing, either, as I recall. For reasons I can't specifically remember, I'd identified Dr. McCoy as my favorite *Star Trek* character at the ripe old age of six. I honestly can't say, at least prior to the date previously stated, when or how I'd been exposed to the science fiction show at that point. Being born in 1972, I obviously missed its original run by a few years, so reruns would have been the only option, but I must have watched it frequently to have so desperately wanted to be a pint-sized version of DeForrest Kelley running around the streets of Greenville panhandling for candy in an acceptable fashion. So, this was my mother's only mission, to assist her first born in finding a Dr. McCoy mask and outfit by October 31st.

Just days prior to Halloween, my mother walked into the kitchen with a shopping bag from somewhere, from one of the Marts, most likely Stein or Magic based on where we lived in Greenville, and proudly announced she'd found my costume. I all but snatched the bag from her and dove into the paper sack and produced a fine piece of Ben Cooper costume craftsmanship—a Mr. Spock mask.

Slightly confused, I looked again in the sack for an accompanying costume, but there was nothing else other than laundry detergent and Twinkies. I asked my mother where the rest of my outfit was, at the moment ignoring the fact that it was a mask of my second favorite character, not my first as previously requested. Her answer bordered somewhere between "This is all I could find," and "I grabbed what I had time to get." Whatever she said in response answered enough why I was holding the plastic visage of Mr. Spock, and not Dr. McCoy in my hand. This also led immediately to figuring out a solution for what a tiny Vulcan Starfleet officer would wear in just a few nights. That was answered by my mother going through my father's dresser and retrieving a blue T-shirt with a torn pocket on the front. Black slacks would not be an issue, I don't think, as I didn't own anything but dress pants until the age of thirteen.

As for the actual Trick or Treating aspect, I remember going to Mrs. Smoke's house next door and her shoveling half of her bowl into my pumpkin and then hitting most of the other houses on our circle, literally McCorkle Circle. And, you know what? Of all the jawas, Spider-Mans, and cowboys I saw that night, I didn't see another single Starfleet officer, although I recall one kid who kept insisting he was Godzilla but rather resembled a Gorn.

The second memory I have regarding the original series pre-1980 is more accurately a collection of reminiscences that began Christmas 1977. Yes, it's not lost on me that the recollections I do have all seem to anchor to specific dates, especially holidays. That was the year Santa left a bicycle under the tree for me, but I pushed past it in hopes what I really wanted would be there. And it was. Not only the Mego *Enterprise* Playset that I'd longed for more than forever, but also the Mego versions of Captain Kirk, Spock, Dr. McCoy, and Scotty. I can see them all very vividly spread out on the floor in the little alcove between our living room and kitchen, ready to take on the evil Water King of whatever planet I pretended my Mego Aquaman was from. I must have also seen "Mirror, Mirror" by this point, because one of my memories is wrapping golden ribbon left over from Christmas around Scotty's and Spock's waist and having Kirk and Bones wallop them, all in the averagely crafted, not so accurately reproduced Enterprise playset's version of the ship's bridge.

Unfortunately, the last memory I have of those fantastic toys isn't the best. For reasons I didn't know then, my father decided that I was spending way too much time playing "make believe" and with "dolls," so they went away. Not conspicuously disappearing or anything so passive aggressively kind as that, but in a grand spectacle of being dumped in a trash can and hauled to the curb just minutes before the trash truck made its rounds. And, of course, I assume to make me a stronger boy, I was made to watch the entire spectacle and threatened to be whipped within an inch of my life if I shed a single tear.

Belt or not, I ran back into the house, tears rolling, and what seemed like hours later, my father found me in my room. Whatever tongue lashings he'd taken from my mother caused him to come forth with an apology, not one of any great note because I barely even remember it. Just that, though, an apology. No explanation for why he'd taken the only thing I'd truly wanted the previous Christmas away from me as he sat beside me and told me it was time we got ready for bed.

We moved from Greenville to Batesville, Arkansas in early 1980. My mother had gotten a new job and my father had one lined up, so my little sister and I were packed along with the Tupperware, my grandmother's collection of Fiesta Glass, and the bike I'd still yet to learn to ride and made the trip. I have impressions of feelings about being in Arkansas, but not a single memory of actually living there until April 8 of that year.

I was in my bedroom in the second house we'd lived in since moving. I sat on the edge of the bed, tears in my eyes. Not tears of sadness or pain, but anger, whatever passes for rage in a nearly eight-year-old child. I held a broom in my hands, and it shook, probably because I was trembling as if I was freezing. I raised the broom into the air and threw it at the window in front of me, screaming, "I'm not afraid of the dark anymore!" The end of the broomstick hit the glass first, shattering the pane outward into the yard.

From that moment until now, I have nearly perfect recall, particularly of the remainder of my childhood as well as my adolescent years. *Star Trek* came on at 10:30 on KATV, Channel 7 out of Little Rock. It was one of the three channels we could get, having left what would become Cable TV behind in Mississippi for whatever the antenna could catch in Arkansas. It came on every weeknight. That was before the late-night wars were really a thing so most stations filled those hours with reruns, either mysteries like *Hawaii Five-0* and *The Rockford Files* or comedies like *I Love Lucy*. I was lucky to be in the foothills of the Ozarks where we had *Star Trek*.

I could probably point out something in every single episode of the original series that impacted or at least contributed to who I am in some way. I was that kind of kid, am still that kind of adult, able to absorb meaningful things from various sources, especially stories filled with characters I enjoy. That enjoyment comes from either identifying with them in some way or at least aspiring to be like them in some way. I definitely felt the latter with the crew of the *Enterprise* and would only later realize I felt the former with one character after a certain episode of the series.

People look at me weirdly when I say that the most important *Star Trek* episode to me personally is one of the most reviled of the series. At least, it is by most die-hard fans. Yes, I am referring to "Spock's Brain." I am not going to defend it as a great example of storytelling, because it's not. Nor am I going to say it is the most faithful to the way the regular cast is usually portrayed, because, again, doesn't hit that mark either. Overall, it's a lackluster episode all told, except for what it taught a nine-year-old that was already lost in a way.

Fitting in is something we all struggle with, whether we realize it or not, at some point in our lives. For me, even in the years I barely recall, feeling like I was a part of anything was foreign, something I rarely achieved. This meant even within my own family. I struggled with finding my place with kids down the street or in a Sunday school class, and especially in my own house.

I spent a lot of time finding other places I could fit in, primarily because the people I met there didn't necessarily speak back or get to say I couldn't belong. I was the definition of 'nose in a book' by third grade, paddled twice for reading when I should have been doing anything but. If it wasn't print, then it was television, having a passion for detective shows very early on. Movies figured in as well, everything from *Casablanca*, my favorite since I watched it at age ten, to *Star Wars*, the Indiana Jones films, and so forth. I found much comfort in imagination, but as is often the case, you can't physically interact with a fictional character without eyebrows raising.

To be accepted meant several things to me. You had to have something others respected, or at the very least needed. You also had to conform, to be like everyone else to a certain degree. Standing out did not lead to fitting in, based on my experience. "Spock's Brain" assisted greatly with one of these issues for me.

The concept that an entire race could not only benefit but require the intelligence of a single person to survive and exist carried significant weight with me. Not only was Spock the right brain for the job for the people of Sigma Draconis VI, they actually sought him out. His intelligence was of such strength, such draw that they literally stole it and made him the most important person in their world, even if it was just his brain. Not only that, but Spock was thought of so highly by his fellow crewmembers that they, particularly Dr. McCoy, went to great lengths to save him, body and all.

As an adult looking back, I understand how this realization of a ten-year-old kid may seem silly, but at the time, and I do clearly remember it as a light bulb moment, it made more sense than anything else. Fortunately, I didn't believe I had to have my brain surgically removed and installed into a computer. I simply needed to take something I was already lauded for at a young age and invest in it fully, make it my brand of sorts. So, I became the brain, the smartest kid in any room I was in. I just didn't say I was, I proved it and if I didn't have the knowledge to prove it when I walked in, I made sure I did before I came back. Just from that silly little conceit in a poorly told *Star Trek* story, I found the beginnings of an identity.

The second aspect of being accepted that I wished I'd followed *Star Trek*'s lead on more was conforming. The diaspora of characters presented in those three seasons spanned race, ideology, and more. Even if many of the episodes ended up with planets joining the Federation or some all-powerful being dying, individuality was on display, from Uhura's mastery of languages to Sulu's swordsmanship.

I struggled with identity in so many ways as a child. And it really, in a way has been literally a lifelong fight for me, but it really started April 8, 1980. I threw a broomstick through a closed window because I was no longer afraid of the dark, and I was adamant and furious about it. Not about being unafraid, but that I even had to make such an announcement. What followed, though, was anticlimactic. My father, who had convinced me four years earlier that he needed to sleep with me in the same bed and proceeded to do so every single night, didn't say anything at all. He just whipped me for breaking the window and never climbed in my bed again. His lack of response along with the fact that he'd been abusing me each night those four years is why I put all those memories away for nearly twenty-five years.

In a way, that subjugation of self drove me even deeper into the world of fiction. It also formed a stronger connection between me and my Halloween alter ego, now my favorite *Trek* character. Spock's struggle between his two genetic halves mirrored a very similar fight I've had with myself, not just about being an abused child who didn't remember for nearly a quarter of century what my father had done. Identity for me has always been a struggle, between the boy that I threw myself into being after April 8, 1980…and the girl, the woman that I feel I have always been, and may have developed into had I not been abused. The comparison for genetics as two warring sides is accurate as well, due to being born with features of both genders, commonly known as intersexed.

I am working on claiming my truest self now. There are complications, issues that present themselves often. I am not completely "out," although that term bothers me as I never should have been "in" to begin with. In living a life as someone you aren't, you owe obligations to others that aren't so simple to walk away from, something else that Spock dealt with throughout the long history of the character, thanks primarily to Mr. Nimoy.

My journey through life with *Star Trek* has been one of moments, stops along the way that made impressions on me like footprints on the moon. The show, though, has also given me something that I never expected, and even though I didn't have this realization until I was an adult, it was a gift granted to a child who just needed to see someone like her…even if she thought she was him at the time.

Mr. Spock was that for me.

Sorella Smith is a published author, editor, publisher, convention panelist and performer. In many ways, Sorella is finally coming into her own, being a transgender woman who, at her own pace, is taking her place in the life she's been living.

ACKNOWLEDGMENTS

When a book like this comes together, I never take for granted the people who back me up and help me make the dream a reality. Strange love a star-woman teaches, yes, but these people taught me much more important things as *Galloping Around the Cosmos* grew and grew.

Ron Hill – When I finally fixed it in my brain what I wanted for the cover for the book, Ron was the only artist I considered. I've only recently gotten to know him, but his art has already warped to the top of my list of collaborators.

Maggie Ryel – When I'm ready to have the print edition formatted, I say things to Maggie like, "What about this?" and "Can you do that?" and she just does it with no indication of difficulty. Every publisher should be blessed with working with such an architect as her.

Gene Roddenberry – The Great Bird of the Galaxy looms over us all, guiding us to a better future. I'm so grateful he brought his creation into the world for me and you to enjoy forever.

ALSO IN THE "MEMORIES FROM TODAY'S GROWN-UP KIDS" SERIES:

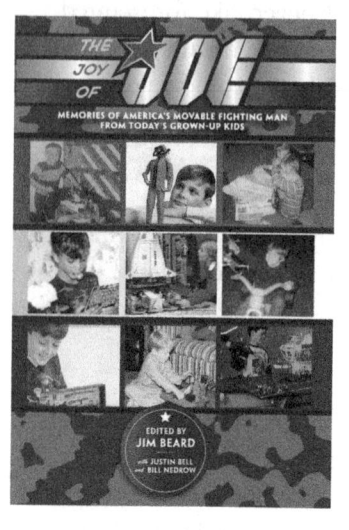

THE JOY OF JOE: MEMORIES OF AMERICA'S MOVABLE FIGHTING MAN FROM TODAY'S GROWN-UP KIDS

"If you grew up as a fan of the 1960s or 1980s versions of GI Joe this is the collection for you...reminiscences that are simultaneously personal and universal no matter your age, location, or childhood experience."
–Amazon Review

RUNNING HOME TO SHADOWS: MEMORIES OF TV'S FIRST SUPERNATURAL SOAP FROM TODAY'S GROWN-UP KIDS

"This book is a great read for fellow Dark Shadows fans. I identified with so many of the thoughts and emotions included in the various essays in this book. Some are funny, some are touching, all are interesting. I highly recommend it!"
–Amazon Review

Available on
AMAZON.COM and
BARNESANDNOBLE.COM

ALSO IN THE "MEMORIES FROM TODAY'S GROWN-UP KIDS" SERIES:

RISING SUN RERUNS: MEMORIES OF JAPANESE TV SHOWS FROM TODAY'S GROWN-UP KIDS

"Outstanding fun read. It'll bring back so many memories of your afternoons after school watching on the old black-and-white television. So well done."
–Amazon Review

D20 OR DIE: MEMORIES OF OLD SCHOOL ROLE-PLAYING GAMES FROM TODAY'S GROWN-UP KIDS

"[The] stories in this book made me laugh, chuckle, think, and almost shed a tear. Reading [them] brought back my own fond memories of gaming sessions from the past."
–Amazon Review

Available on
AMAZON.COM and
BARNESANDNOBLE.COM

ALSO AVAILABLE FROM
Becky BOOKS

ZLONK! ZOK! ZOWIE! THE SUBTERRANEAN BLUE GROTTO ESSAYS ON BATMAN '66 – SEASON ONE

"Great collection of essays about the show. Educational, informative, and fun, *ZLONK! ZOK! ZOWIE!* is a must read for any Batman fan."
–Amazon Review

BIFF! BAM! EEE-YOW! THE SUBTERRANEAN BLUE GROTTO ESSAYS ON BATMAN '66 – SEASON TWO

"Some of the essays are comedic, some filled with trivia, and some are heartfelt reminisces. A truly enjoyable read from cover to cover."
–Amazon Review

OOOFF! BOFF! SPLATT! THE SUBTERRANEAN BLUE GROTTO ESSAYS ON BATMAN '66 – SEASON THREE

"I loved this collection of essays about the final Batman '66 slate of episodes. An enormous thank you to Jim Beard & Co. for giving me an excuse to re-watch the whole show again…"
–Goodreads Review

Available on
AMAZON.COM

ALSO AVAILABLE FROM
Becky BOOKS

D.C. JONES AND ADVENTURE COMMAND INTERNATIONAL

"A fun pulp read that felt just like it's meant to feel: Playing with action figures, uncovering mysteries, taking out bad guys with skill and brains. It's a joy and I look forward to the sequels."
–Amazon Review

D.C. JONES AND ADVENTURE COMMAND INTERNATIONAL 2

"The tone of the stories in this volume strikes a perfect balance between action and character, and Beard skillfully gives each member of the Adventure Command distinct and easily identifiable personalities. [The] prose keeps the stories moving at a good clip with snappy dialogue and plenty of action."
–Amazon Review

D.C. JONES AND ADVENTURE COMMAND INTERNATIONAL 3

"Jim Beard once again takes readers on a globe-trotting adventure that pushes his team of heroes to their limits against a foe whose capabilities are far superior to their own."
–Amazon Review

Available on
AMAZON.COM

Made in the USA
Middletown, DE
04 May 2024